COMMON SENSE
ABOUT
PSYCHOANALYSIS

Other Books by Rudolph Wittenberg

Adolescence and Discipline 1959

On Call for Youth 1955

The Art of Group Discipline 1951

So You Want to Help People: A Mental Hygiene
Primer for Group Leaders 1947

Hasenheide 19 1934

COMMON SENSE
ABOUT
PSYCHOANALYSIS

Rudolph Wittenberg

DOUBLEDAY & COMPANY, INC.

GARDEN CITY, NEW YORK

1962

Acknowledgments

I have had the help of friends and colleagues in the writing of this book. David Klein suggested it in the first place and saw it through to the final draft. Anne Freedgood, tireless editor at Doubleday, worked with me patiently through every draft.

I have had valuable assistance with the controversial chapters, particularly those on the training and background of analysts. I want to express particular gratitude to Dr. Henry Lowenfeld and Dr. Lawrence Kubie, training analysts of the New York Psychoanalytic Institute; Dr. Daniel Shapiro, training analyst of the Columbia University Psychoanalytic Clinic; and Dr. Florence Halpern, a clinical psychologist prominent in the struggle for the certification of psychologists. C532930

Among the readers of the complete manuscript, I am very much indebted to Drs. Milton and Hanna Kapit, psychoanalysts; Francis Bartlett, a psychotherapist; Jeanette Weinandy, a social worker; Dr. Lester Shapiro, a physician; and Dr. George Musa, a surgeon. My wife, Diana, stood up well throughout the many changes, with good critical observations. There have been excellent comments from Helen Wittenberg, a mathematician; Marion Lehman, an artist; James Perlstein, a historian; and Jean Shapiro, a housing administrator.

For the secretarial work, I am grateful, as in the past, to Kohana Wiles.

Table of Contents

Introduction

The theory and practice of psychoanalysis, developed by Sigmund Freud more than half a century ago, have had a profound effect on the thinking of this century. Psychoanalysis has deeply influenced education, the arts, literature, medicine, psychology, and social work. It is freely discussed, joked about, worshiped, and despised, but it is actually no more understood than Einstein's relativity theory, another great scientific discovery that everybody has heard about.

This book is an attempt to talk common sense about psychoanalysis. It tries to answer the questions that the author has most often been asked about his work: What is psychoanalysis really? What goes on during an analysis? How long does an analysis usually take? Why does it cost so much? Should everyone have an analysis if he can? What should an analysis do for a person? How does a person get to be a psychoanalyst?—and many other sensible questions about which there are a great many popular misconceptions. If the reader should at times suffer from the "medical student's disease" and discover in himself all the symptoms described in the book, he must remember that these are not "case histories" but constructs based on fragments of the characters of former patients, who are so disguised that no real person is recognizable any longer. Any similarities between real patients, the illustrations in this book, and the readers are purely coincidental.

Occasionally, I have referred to another book or a study or an organization. I have not used footnotes, but have listed titles at the end of the book. This is in keeping with the spirit of the book, which is not a primer or a textbook but an attempt to share the pleasure and excitement of one of the most significant developments to date in the art and science of understanding people.

COMMON SENSE
ABOUT
PSYCHOANALYSIS

ONE

·

What Is Psychoanalysis?

Psychoanalysis is both a form of psychotherapy—that is, a method of treatment for certain kinds of emotional sickness—and a research tool. Although these two functions are related, they can be discussed separately. In this book, psychoanalysis will be discussed only as a treatment method, not as a method for investigating psychological processes.

What kind of treatment method is psychoanalysis?

The New International Dictionary gives this definition:

> Psychoanalysis is the method developed by Sigmund Freud for analyzing the content and mechanisms of a person's mental life, for purposes of psychotherapy. By dream analysis and similar devices it aids the patient to discover and relive his unconscious memories and to adjust his mental conflicts.

Before we spell out this very condensed statement, it might be well to make it quite clear what psychoanalysis is not. It is not a philosophy of life or a method of solving social problems, although many of its ardent enthusiasts have tried to make it both these things. It is not even a cure-all for all mental conflicts and all people. Just as surgery or one of the "miracle drugs" is recommended for some forms of physical sickness and not for others, so psychoanalysis is useful only in certain kinds of mental or emotional disturbances.

The one large area of mental illness in which psychoanalysis is perhaps the best form of treatment is the category of the neuroses. There are a great many kinds of neuroses, but even if one could list them all, basically no two neuroses are the same, just as no two human beings are the same.

In its most generalized form, neurosis is a clinical term that describes a condition in which an individual is forced to use parts of his mental energy to cope with drives and impulses from his early childhood. Ideally, infantile drives are successfully integrated into the growing personality. But in some people this is only partially accomplished. Some of the early drives return—often during adolescence or later in life—at a time when the individual is otherwise fully grown and in control of himself. He then has to use parts of his energy to cope with these early instinctual demands instead of directing his whole effort toward the adult goals he has set for himself: to learn, to work, to get along with people, to love and to marry, and to fulfill his ambitions as completely as possible. This inability to be in full charge of one's energy represents a painful state of inner conflict. It is the core of the neurosis.

There will be many illustrations of neurotic conflicts throughout this book, but to clarify the term at the beginning, let us take an oversimplified example:

One of every individual's very early drives is the desire to remain as closely attached as possible to the source of nurture—his mother. A young scientist apparently had overcome this early need to a high degree throughout his childhood. By the time he reached high school, his first neurotic symptoms appeared—when his parents went out in the evening he experienced increasing feelings of fear, and later of panic. Since he was a very intelligent and otherwise mature young man, he was ashamed of his symptoms and hid them from everybody. He wished his parents a pleasant evening, and as soon as he was alone, he experienced the identical feeling of desertion that he had felt when his mother left him, as a little boy, to go to the store. He did not remember these early desertion fears consciously, but memories of them later returned from his unconscious mind, during his analysis. His fears became so severe that he could neither sleep nor work. Night sounds became nightmares to him; shadows from the lights of passing cars seemed to be monsters. He found that when he went to bed and wrapped the blanket tightly around him, he felt better. Often he relieved his anxiety by masturbation, which he repeated until he fell asleep from exhaustion.

In time, he discovered that the presence of another person reduced his fear considerably, and he arranged to have friends sleep over or he would stay at the home of one of his many friends. Gradually the fear of being alone at night left him, only to be replaced by a new symptom—he found it difficult to eat in the company of other people. Although it may seem contradictory, this problem was related to the same early drives to remain part of his first love object, his mother, who had also been the source of food. Unknown to him until the analytic process revealed his early memories of feeding, he had throughout his childhood tried so hard to keep his mother near him that he had forced himself to eat whatever she gave him, whether he liked it or not. His mother had been very concerned with food and always emphasized the importance of it; she watched him eat and made sure that he finished his plate every time. He never had admitted it to himself, but he hated to be watched by his mother, and tried to free himself from her rigid inspection. Secretly he was very angry at his mother, and on a few rare occasions allowed himself the admission of hostile thoughts. Nearly twenty years later, he suddenly found the company of other people—particularly close friends who cared about him—unbearable. He did not mind eating with strangers who did not watch him and had no interest in his food, but when he had to eat with friends, he suffered from severe anxiety.

Again, he managed to cope with this symptom by eating alone whenever possible, and in time succeeded in overcoming to some extent his aversion to being watched. However, when he had his first job offer, in a city some five hundred miles from his parents' home, he found himself unable to accept it. As with the fear of being alone and the conflict over eating with friends, he was extremely uncomfortable and did not admit to anybody that he could not take an excellent job because it was too far from home. He did not even admit it to himself completely, but found other good and plausible excuses for turning the job down. In time, he found another job in his home town and forgot about his neurotic anxieties. He did not face up to his neurosis until a new symptom interfered so powerfully with his conscious wishes that he considered his conflicts in earnest. This symptom, which finally brought him to analysis, was his inability to form close and satisfying relationships with people, most particularly with young women. Remembering his adolescent night panics and his pain while eating with friends, he had trained himself to become what he called "independent." As soon as a relationship became intimate, he withdrew, sometimes with odd explanations. Usually he fell back on the importance of his scientific work, but actually he was lonely and hungry for close relationships.

He was unable to use his mental energy to accomplish what he really wanted. Some of his early drives had not been successfully integrated into his total personality. They had returned and forced him to use his energy to cope with them, instead of with his realistic life goals. He was deadlocked in a powerful internal battle.

As I said earlier, this illustration is vastly oversimplified—I have omitted a great many significant clinical aspects. However, the sketch may clarify what we meant by the more abstract definition of neurosis, the form of mental illness that can often be cured by psychoanalysis.

In the case of the young scientist, as in the case of many neurotic patients, his basic sense of self-preservation was disturbed. In one way or another, he was not able to act in his best interest. This disruption may manifest itself in various ways: It may appear as a reduction of work capacity, such as is seen in gifted students who function far below their potential ability even though they spend more time studying than other students. It may show in a constant tiredness without any organic cause, or in the choice of a profession or occupation that does no justice to the person's gifts. This kind of behavior, in which somebody is clearly being unfair to himself, is another manifestation of the lack of self-preservation. One might call it *self-injury*. Other expressions of it are the lack of proper care of oneself: taking chances while driving, or trying dangerous stunts. It appears more subtly in a propensity to form relationships that are not good for one, relationships in which one will get hurt. These may be friendships or marriages. Classic illustrations are the class clown; the man who is always somebody's patsy; and the woman who has so hidden her intelligence that she has convinced herself and others that she is uninteresting and dull.

Lack of self-preservation may also show up in an individual's inability to love. The young scientist mentioned before is an obvious example. A less obvious case is the man who says he loves his wife, and is a faithful husband and a good provider, but still does not really understand his wife, her needs, or her way of looking at the world. This man cannot love with any degree of objectivity, and will be unable to understand any people close to him. Like a small child, he will use his wife and friends as a mirror for himself. He will be dependent on them, and he will fulfill his obligations faithfully, but he will never be able to sense what they experience.

This same difficulty with what is called "object love" may reveal itself in the sexual life of some individuals. There may be an inability to accept the other sex, in spite of intercourse or marriage. Sexual life may be an ordeal or an obligation, a humdrum release of physical tensions or a routine procedure like having certain meals on certain days, but it will never be a real satisfaction, perhaps because of an inability to co-ordinate tenderness and passion, rather like that of adolescence. It may appear in such symptoms as full or partial frigidity or a failure to achieve any real release, or in conditional satisfaction, when excitement depends on fantasies, touching of objects, special clothes or sadistic-masochistic love play. (In the latter cases, it is the dependence on these special conditions that characterizes them as perversions.)

Inversions of sexual instincts may be expressed in partial revulsion toward one's partner's or one's own body parts, or in the choice of partners of one's own sex. In all these situations, the individual is not able to use his energies to get the satisfactions he really wants.

Lack of self-interest may also show in the way a person expresses his aggressive instincts—excessive fantasies may prevent him from expressing his aggression in its most elementary form. Saying no, or disagreeing with certain significant people, is impossible for some individuals, who try to please others and then torture themselves secretly and for a long time for not having spoken their minds. Or they may suffer from the opposite—from inappropriate and repetitious aggressiveness; disagreeing on principle, as it were, with everybody and anything. Then again, there may be rapid alternations between submission and hostility, followed by abject apologies or defiant self-assertion.

Other people whose sense of self-preservation is disturbed find it very difficult to react appropriately to any stimulus, and overreact to everything. They are people who cannot take anything in their stride. Ordinary tensions rapidly become unbearable; waiting is nearly impossible; overexcitement, or overreaction to disappointments, is not the exception but the norm for this personality. Parallel to them are the people who apparently experience no reaction at all to events.

Excessive fantasy is another way in which self-preservation disturbances show. It may be expressed in more serious thinking disorders, such as the continuous belief that I am a fraud or that I will be discovered for what I really am—a hideous, villainous creature. Another very painful way in which this kind of fantasy may be expressed is, too much success is dangerous and therefore I must be careful not to do well or to outdo a potential competitor or rival.

A person in this category may be completely convinced that he or she is ugly or lacks any kind of intelligence—so much so that he will laugh at people who assure him that he is attractive or intelligent. Some people are convinced that the cards are stacked against them and there is no use reversing fate; others are equally certain that they are born lucky and protected against all ills. They fantasy that they possess magical powers with which they control their lives and those of others. For them, everything hinges on this power, and they feel guilty if somebody near them has some trouble, because it is "my fault."

Another common form of fantasy is the assumption that one knows what others are thinking or feeling and, knowing it, can safely act on this assumption. Some people are always certain that they understand a situation, whereas actually they rarely do. They see what they want to see in another person's face or in the newspaper. Their opposites are the people who are sure that they never know what is going on or what somebody is saying, and keep on asking for explanations, while they really have, all along, perceived what is going on. The point is that they do not believe that they understand, but must continue to doubt and to question themselves and others. By the time a neurosis is fully developed, the doubts and the fantasies are so automatic that the individual does not recognize them as fantasies any more. At moments he glimpses his neurosis in feelings of distress and even panic. At other moments he tells himself that whatever is troubling him is "normal," requires no attention, and will be settled by time and patience.

In some ways, he is right. Everybody is troubled by some of the symptoms I have sketched out, at least occasionally. No one of these symptoms is significant by itself. It is the degree of these manifestations and the manner in which they are combined that matter. The young scientist, for example, had suffered from several neurotic symptoms for quite a few years without taking them seriously enough to consult anybody. When the fear of isolation interlocked with the anxiety about eating with friends and connected with the impossibility of taking a desirable job, and when all of these symptoms led him to recognize that he could not get close to people, he experienced acute pain and discomfort, and consulted an analyst.

But even this illustration does not tell us anything about the intensity of neurotic symptoms, or the practically unlimited ways in which they may manifest themselves. It is not possible to categorize types of neurotic disturbances; it is possible only to indicate some of the more clear-cut manifestations.

Only a competent analyst can decide whether or not analysis is indicated for a given individual. Freud made it clear early in his work that the uncovering of unconscious mechanisms requires a certain state of health, contradictory as this may seem. It takes courage and resilience to face aspects of one's character that one has tried to ignore. The young scientist who tried to forget about his desertion fears during his high-school days, and his later anxiety about eating with people, needed considerable honesty with himself, and enough strength to come back to these and other humiliating feelings and face up to them in the process of analysis.

The ability to face one's problems, the readiness to see an analyst four times a week for several years, the financial sacrifice required, are all indicators of strength and of the healthy parts of the personality. It is this health that is needed to cope with inner disturbances.

Health and illness are not absolutes, but coexist in every organism. It is realistic to think of them in terms of degrees. When somebody has a cold but no temperature, we don't consider him a sick man, even though he has an infection. If he develops a high fever and the cold becomes pneumonia, we say that he is ill.

It is the same with mental health and illness. We can usually cope with some of our inner disturbances, even though they may represent aspects of a neurosis. When the disturbances interfere with many aspects of our lives, we consider them a form of illness. But even in the most extreme form of mental illness, the psychoses, there are still healthy and sound areas of the mind. Edward Glover, a British analyst, has suggested that we "are all larval psychotics," making it clear that in certain circumstances a healthy person can become very, very sick. Most clinicians would agree that the difference between neurosis and psychosis is a matter of degree.

The over-all classification "neurotic" is a form of naïveté that does no justice either to the person who makes it or to the person to whom it is applied. This kind of labeling is often done by people who are fiercely determined to appear "normal" and who deny that anything is wrong with them. They resemble the people who deny obvious physical disturbances as long as they can, and put off seeing their physician, sometimes until they have become desperately sick. By the same token, those suffering from serious emotional problems consider it quite unthinkable that their fierce determination masks a serious condition that requires therapy. The denial of illness is as much a symptom of neurosis as its opposite, the well-known attitude called hypochondria. Both are exaggerated attitudes.

It is not unusual to find people in analysis who have been treated for some time and still deny to themselves that they are not completely well. These people take one very obvious and undeniable symptom and make believe that this is all that is wrong with them. An intelligent and attractive woman in her thirties, for example, used her insomnia in this way. She had tried medication for years and was afraid that she might become addicted to drugs. After having gone to physicians for most of her adult life and being told that what she needed was analysis, she finally went to an analyst. She did not consider herself ill or emotionally disturbed in the least. All she felt she needed was some relief from her insomnia and her tortuous nightmares. Otherwise, she said, she was fine.

As she talked to the analyst, she described serious difficulties with her superiors in her work; she mentioned, in passing, that she was about to enter her third marriage; she earned a good salary as a university instructor, but she was deeply in debt and could not, as she put it, hold on to money. She spent too much on liquor and travel. Her apartment was too expensive, and so were her clothes, but this was the way she was, she declared. She was

1

as right as rain and well adjusted in all respects—except for the "nuisance of sleeping." Perhaps one could consider her "neurotic" —and she pronounced this word with antiseptic quotation marks —but was this not better than a dull, ordinary "middle-class" existence?

This patient had no clear awareness of the nature of her inner conflicts. Since she was successful in so many ways, it was hard for her to come to terms with her neurosis. But once she had made up her mind to use her determination and intelligence to face and resolve her inner conflicts, she worked at her analysis with the same dedication and persistence that had made her doctoral thesis and her lectures so successful.

What made the beginning of her analysis difficult for her was the necessity of re-experiencing feelings from the past and recognizing how these unconscious feelings interfered with the present. Used to thinking in abstractions and ideas, this patient, like many others, was at first impatient with the analyst's inquiry into details of her experiences.

When she declared that her mother had been "domineering," the analyst asked how this had been expressed. When the patient said that her mother never let her buy her own clothes, the analyst wanted to know how old the patient had been when this situation existed. Once the approximate age range had been recalled, there were further inquiries into details of a given shopping trip to a given store. Recalling more and more details made the forgotten experiences more and more vivid and exposed the partially covered memories. This was of course much more cumbersome than saying "Mother was domineering"; it aroused a good deal of annoyance on the patient's part, but it made it possible for her to recognize experiences, feelings, thoughts, and drives from the past. Before one can give up vague fantasies or unconscious drives from the distant past, one has to be able to see and fully recognize them, with conscious awareness. This is accomplished through the process of reliving these early feelings.

The necessity of reliving, as one of the characteristics of psychoanalysis, makes this method of treatment different from all others. And it explains why intellectual understanding does not suffice. If this were enough, practitioners of psychoanalysis could study it in the classroom and laboratory and then be able to practice it themselves, as is the case in all other methods of treatment. No physician is required to experience surgery on his own body before he can qualify as a surgeon. Psychoanalysts, however, are required to experience psychoanalysis of their own psyche before they even begin to study the theory and technique of it.

This idea of reliving has been responsible for a great deal of misunderstanding and confusion about psychoanalysis as a whole, because the process of reliving has to be experienced to be really understood. It is based on Freud's exploration of the unconscious, and it is accomplished through what is called free association. In the next chapter, the process of free association will be discussed more fully. Here, it is enough to state that the reliving of past experiences does not mean, as is often erroneously assumed, a preoccupation with the past.

The process of reliving experiences that no longer exist on the conscious level, and are therefore not reachable by reason, does not mean "digging" into the past or talking primarily about things past. In order to appreciate this seeming contradiction, it is necessary to recognize one psychoanalytic finding—the fact that time is a function of the conscious, rational mind and has no meaning in the unconscious. This is illustrated by dreams. While we know with our conscious mind that we went to bed at a given time, we do not know that we are in bed, or what time it is, as our unconscious mind produces the complex dramas or stories we partially recall upon awakening. In dreams, events of the day before are experienced in a setting that we knew twenty years before; characters whom we met today appear together with characters whom we loved or hated in our earliest childhood.

While the passage of time is absolute, we use it in everyday language simply as a convenient measurement for the various phases that result from the rotation of the earth around the sun. It is not surprising, then, that it has no place in the unconscious mind. Since the reliving of the past, which is basic to psychoanalysis, concerns itself mainly with the unconscious or partly conscious part of the mind, time is not relevant. Therefore, reliving past experiences does not necessarily mean talking about infancy or childhood. The patient may talk about anything that comes to his mind.

The question of time, in a different sense, brings up the frequently asked question of how long an analysis takes. People say that they have been in analysis for three years. Aside from the fact that the phrase "in analysis" is sometimes used rather vaguely, because not every therapeutic experience is analysis, as we shall see, the question of length is not clear because the phrase "three years" does not describe the number of analytic hours. The patient who sees his analyst three times a week will, after three years, have had approximately four hundred analytic hours. In terms of work weeks, using a forty-hour week as the norm, he will have worked some ten weeks in the analytic office, which is very different from his impression that he has been "in analysis for three years."

The most reasonable measure for the length of analysis is the analytic, fifty-minute hour. A survey undertaken in Great Britain by practicing analysts averaged about eight hundred hours for a complete analysis. Another estimate, made by the American Psychoanalytic Association, came to about seven hundred hours for students in analytic training, who must first have a complete analysis, like any other patient. Based on these two surveys, it would be realistic to think of seven to eight hundred hours as the average length of a complete analysis. Since most American analysts have adopted the four-times-a-week practice, and usually take a month's vacation, the eight hundred hours are spread out over four to five years.

However, there are many unpredictable factors that may lengthen or shorten the total process: Some people learn the method of free association in a relatively short time, others need many more months. Unconscious feelings may be deeply buried and covered over with layers of rationalization. It takes much longer for some people to give up their idealized self-image than for others. Sometimes the patient's family complicates the process of analysis and prolongs it; in other cases, the family is most co-operative and may help to shorten it. The depth of the patient's fear of changing, his readiness to give up neurotic satisfactions, and other, similar factors have to be weighed before one can arrive at a sound estimate of the time required to complete a given analysis.

One of the major reasons for asking about the length of an analysis is concern over the expense. With twenty to thirty dollars a session the current analytic fee among most American analysts, it is very clear why people want to know how long such an expense will continue. While this question, too—like most of the others touched upon in this first chapter—will be taken up more fully later in the book, we might as well face the fact from the start that the cost of analysis prevents many people from considering it, even after they have overcome all of their other objections. The total expense of a full analysis is also one of the reasons why short cuts and less costly substitutes are being sought. It is true that there are clinics; it is true that people not infrequently increase their earning power as a result of an analysis; and it is true that the analyst who can see only one patient per hour charges less for his services than many dentists. Nevertheless, the fact remains that a full analysis takes many hours and requires a considerable outlay of money.

The answer does not, I believe, lie in diluting a first-rate method of treatment—because there are no short cuts—but in the increased public awareness of the overriding significance of mental health. There is a Mental Health Act, and there is a very recent, honest, and shocking Congressional report on the state of our mental health as a nation. There are, in the private field, hopeful signs of recognition of mental illness. Insurance companies have begun to take notice of psychotherapy in general. Perhaps it is not too much to dream of the day when psychoanalysis will be accessible to those who need it, whether they are rich or poor.

TWO

·

Free Association

The dictionary definition of psychoanalysis cited at the beginning of the preceding chapter states that psychoanalysis works through "dream analysis and similar devices" toward the adjustment of mental conflicts. The most important of these "similar devices" is the specific manner of communication in the analytic process. It is known as free association.

In associating freely, the patient says anything that comes to mind. People who have had an analysis know how difficult this deceptively simple-sounding task actually is. Contrary to popular opinion, the task of saying anything that comes to mind is insurmountable for some people, hard work for others, and easy for nobody. Yet free association is the transmission belt of communication between analyst and patient.

The difficulty stems not merely from the usual hesitation about sharing ideas and feelings with a stranger. This initial reluctance is overcome in time and is not specific to psychoanalytic communication. What is really complicated is the necessity of giving up a way of thinking and expressing oneself that has taken many years to acquire—that is, conscious control over one's utterances and a logical manner of relating facts and feelings. From the babble of early infancy to the slow acquisition of words and the gradual mastery of language—via the process of imitation—the human being learns the habit of "talking sense." Parents and teachers spend years training children to think before they speak, to avoid rambling and incoherent ideas. In school and college, students are praised for precision and continuity. Throughout life, men strive for clear, organized communication. By the time a person begins analysis, this orderly and accustomed way of speaking has usually become natural.

In analysis, quite suddenly and without any special training, the patient is asked to say anything that comes to mind, regardless of his feelings of shame or embarrassment, or whether the thought or feeling seems important or not. He is asked to keep the control gates down for fifty minutes several times a week and let out anything that happens to flow across the surface of his mind; to avoid censorship, concern with content and direction, and all deliberate and purposeful control of his speech. In short, he is asked to do the very opposite of what he has learned—not to choose what makes immediate sense, not to talk to the point, not to select or keep watch over what he is saying.

The process of learning to abide by this basic rule—which is, as a matter of fact, the only rule of psychoanalysis—is part of the therapy. By the gradual elimination of conscious tendencies in verbal communication, the not fully conscious part of the mind becomes accessible to observation. Slowly the patient discovers that in free association, too, there is selection, a different kind of order of continuity than the one he is accustomed to—the complicated structure of the preconscious and unconscious parts of the mind. He realizes that the sequence of associations makes a kind of sense after all, that unexplained thoughts and feelings, "left-of-field" memories, and seemingly wild impulses all add up after a while. A new dimension of the inner world emerges which gives the patient pause before discharging impulses. A person accustomed to acting on impulse discovers that in the analytic process nothing is acted on. This is one of the important safeguards in learning to give up conscious control over verbal communication: everything should be expressed, but nothing is acted out.

Another difficulty in learning to say anything that comes to mind is the fact that the analyst does not always respond to the patient's utterances. All of us are used to a certain pattern of communication throughout our lives. When we speak to somebody, we usually get a response. When we ask a question, we ordinarily get an answer. When we are angry, we expect the other person to react in some way. When we express feelings of any kind, we are used to hearing an echo from our fellow man. This is not necessarily the case in analytic communication. The analyst often has to listen for a very long time before he can speak. This is not simply because, as in all situations, one has to understand before one can help; it is determined by the analytic process itself. The analyst is not there to react the way people usually do when we speak to them but to remain open with all his senses, conscious and unconscious, to the associations of the patient. His role is, as Freud put it, to be the piece of white paper on which the patient can write his associations.

The more unobtrusive the analyst remains, the better for the patient's flow of associations. The analyst listens with free-floating attention, absorbing and trying to put together the many pieces of the puzzle. He has been trained to associate to his patient's associations and to use his clinical judgment about when to intervene or to interpret. When to interpret and in what way is part of this clinical judgment, based on many years of scientific training in the theory and practice of this treatment method.

This sounds reasonable enough, but it is often very distressing to the patient who expects—in spite of his intellectual knowledge—the same response to his expressions that he would get from a sympathetic friend. Because everybody likes to repeat the familiar—by definition—the patient tries to make his new experience appear familiar. After a short time, he will try to relate the behavior of the analyst to the behavior of people he has known before. If, for example, he had a father who did not talk much, who was very busy and could not be disturbed by his children, the analyst's silence will remind him of his father. This is a perfectly natural process, which we are used to in everyday behavior. The analyst in this case will seem like his father. The patient will once more feel angry and frustrated at the silence, as he felt long ago. He will begin to relive some experiences of the past in the present process of psychoanalysis. If he is not interrupted, he will find himself expressing his anger in a manner that was not permitted by his father when the patient was a child. As he associates freely, he will feel emotions and think ideas that he himself did not know he had in his mind. Everything that was censored in the past will gradually emerge, and occasionally the analyst will be able to break his silence and make an interpretation of the jumbled associations that may connect feelings of the day before with feelings from earliest childhood. Suddenly some very puzzling piece of behavior, or a very disturbing feeling connected with the patient's job or marriage, will make sense.

Some of the feelings and ideas from the depth of the unconscious mind emerge in this way and illuminate current behavior. To illustrate this, let us take a very small slice from an analytic session of a young and successful executive. One of the many difficulties that troubled him sufficiently to make him consider analysis was his complete inability to form any meaningful relationships with other people. Although he got along with people superficially, he was in reality isolated, had no real friends and no woman about whom he cared deeply. Yet he was hungry for friendship and hoped one day to marry.

He had trouble associating freely because he was fearful lest some of his unacceptable feelings about himself and others come out against his will. He did talk in his sessions, but it was an orderly, controlled report of his thinking and activity. The analyst was aware of the fact that the patient could not allow himself to feel or to express feelings in the session—the very difficulty that prevented him from having meaningful relationships. However, since the analyst was trained to pay close attention to the manner in which his patients talk—aside from what they say—he picked up one significant word that the patient used frequently when talking about people. The word was "stupid." When he said this, he clearly did not mean that the person to whom he was referring was not intelligent or not educated, but what he did mean was hidden from the analyst until one session. C532930

Part of the flow of associations during this session went as follows: ". . . I went to this party of Warner's and it was as usual . . . lots of people . . . stupid talk and too many drinks. . . . I didn't stay too late because we had this important client the next day and I wanted to be rested . . . some trouble falling asleep . . . don't know what makes me think of this but had a letter from my little nephew, my brother's second child. . . . I like him a lot, one of my favorite people . . . saw him for the holidays and oh, yes, there was this thing with that stupid aunt. . . . She would coo and fuss over that little boy and then pinch his cheeks and he cried and that woman slobbered all over him. . . ."

ANALYST (*interrupting*): You sound as if *you* had been cooed over and got angry. . . .

PATIENT: It was like that. It reminded me of my mother's best friend, another stupid woman, who would always bring me presents and kiss me and squeeze my legs and pinch me. It was disgusting. The presents she used to bring were always very educational—she was some kind of professor of education—but my little nephew must have felt as I did. . . .

ANALYST: This friend of your mother's was a professor of education?

PATIENT: Something like that, lots of book learning.

ANALYST: When you called her "stupid" you didn't mean uneducated. You meant insensitive.

PATIENT (*after a pause*): Yeah, that's right—insensitive, that's what she was.

ANALYST: And perhaps you usually mean "insensitive" when you say "stupid." You use this word quite a bit.

PATIENT (*slowly*): I guess I really do. I guess I'm saying that a lot of people are insensitive. . . . (*Pause*)

ANALYST: What comes to your mind now?

PATIENT: For some reason, I am suddenly very annoyed at you. Something about this last conversation bothers me. . . . What's the matter with calling people stupid? . . . So I mean insensitive . . . it's true, isn't it? People are insensitive . . . they don't give a damn . . . they don't care. . . .

ANALYST: But all along you have said that it was you who couldn't get close to people. . . .

This was probably the first time that the patient experienced his inner conflicts. His intellectual, "non-stupid" explanations of his behavior had not helped him but continued to keep his fears of people alive. As he began to associate in this session, some feelings of anger emerged, and the anger was directed against the analyst. At the end of the session, the patient was on the verge of discovering that it was he who was insensitive, for reasons that had still to emerge from the unconscious part of the mind.

Just as the contradiction in his thinking was coming to the surface, the patient experienced anger at the analyst. He was not quite ready to accept this interpretation of himself, and defended his old way of behaving with an outburst. The interpretation the analyst suggested interfered with the picture he had of himself, his self-image.

At what he judges to be the proper point in the analysis, the analyst "plays back" some of the associations the patient has produced, and in hearing them the patient experiences the peculiar sensation that the analyst is not repeating what he himself has said, but is talking about somebody else, only distantly related. It sounds different and sometimes positively foreign. He has held up a mirror, and the patient does not like what he sees. It conflicts with his self-image.

He may reject the mental image, just as all of us frequently reject pictorial images of ourselves and blame the photographer when the picture does not flatter us. But how do we develop our image of ourselves in the first place, and how do we know what we look like or are like?

The formation of the self-image follows a long and winding road, fraught with distortions all along the way. To mention only one important one: part of our self-image is derived from the way significant love objects—like parents or meaningful friends—need to see us. If a parent, for example, has a very definite idea of what the child should look like or be like—perhaps even before it is born—he will try to shape the child in this image, and the child, trying to conform to his parents' idea of him, may form a "self"-image that does not really reflect his personality at all. To some extent, everybody is influenced by the wishes and demands of the people around him, but sometimes, when these demands are too strong a contrast to inner demands, serious personality conflicts may ensue, leading to the development of neurotic character traits.

Even where the parents' views of their children are relatively objective, the child's self-image will become distorted by ideals, by the child's choice of desirable figures to model himself on, by the ways in which his instincts cope with the demands of civilization, by the pressure of the culture in which we live, and many other factors.

When the analyst makes an interpretation of the patient's character, based on the material the patient has given him, the patient's acceptance or rejection of the interpretation depends, among other things, on his self-image. If he does not like the picture he is shown, he is apt to feel that the analyst did not listen well. He is annoyed and withdraws from the analyst, becoming critical or even hostile. Perhaps he may feel vindictive enough to try to pay the analyst back by not associating, by saying nothing. He may pout or even cry at the seemingly unfair image the analyst presents to him.

The patient is now in the midst of re-experiencing feelings from the past. He is in analysis. While he is in this state of re-experiencing, he is not fully aware of the fact that the analyst is a trained clinician, a doctor whom he is paying—and who is not interested in hurting anyone's vanity. The patient feels exactly as he felt long ago, and by continuing to associate more and more freely, he uncovers aspects of his personality that have lodged in his unconscious and interfered with the fullest enjoyment of living.

One of the things that comes to the patient's mind as he associates freely is his dreams. In a way, they are the freest associations of all, for they were produced, without the censorship of the conscious mind, during sleep.

Before discussing the use of dreams in analysis, it may be

helpful to clarify a few things about dreams in general. It is commonly believed that psychoanalysis operates on the assumption that dreams have easy, pat, universal interpretations; that Freud assigned certain meanings to certain symbols, so that to dream of, say, a snake, the ocean, a skyscraper, an automobile, or a hole in the ground always has one definite, sexual meaning. Although this may make for an entertaining party game, it has no more relation to psychoanalysis than the toy doctor kits for five-year-olds have to the bag physicians carry on house calls.

In the original German edition of Freud's works, the second and third volumes, which come to seven hundred pages, are devoted to "The Interpretation of Dreams," and the seventh chapter alone often serves as the text for one or two semesters of intensive study in universities and analytic-training institutes. Even this represents only a fraction of Freud's writing on dreams, which in turn is only a fraction of the intensive literature of scientific writing on dreams by many other authors. The study of dreams has a high priority in the study of psychoanalysis and usually runs through the whole four-year course, beginning with Freud's introductory lectures and going on to more and more complicated issues of dream interpretation. It is probably the most complicated area of psychoanalytic study, and subject to continuous research.

Dreams have their own language, which cannot be translated into understandable, everyday meaning without a special dictionary. The dictionary is the patient's free associations, not the analyst's speculations or ramblings. Without the free associations, one does not know what events, from the day before the dream, were used for dream tapestry; one cannot connect present and past, or understand what emotions are being expressed, relative to the analysis. The so-called "wishes" that people assume are visible in dreams are derivatives of the instinctual life, perhaps of earliest infancy—since time does not operate in memory and

dreams—expressed in current language. Phrases are used literally
—"being in hot water" is translated into sitting in a bathtub of
warm water—for reasons not immediately obvious.

Some of the complexities may be illustrated through a very
short dream of a young woman in analysis. The dream was: "I
am in analysis. As I get up from the couch, you hand me a blue
cape, put it around my shoulders, and I walk out."

Nobody could translate this dream without the patient's free
associations. Where did the idea of a cape come from? Why does
the analyst put it around the patient's shoulders? What is the
whole dream about, and how does it connect with other associations at this phase of her analysis?

Neither patient nor analyst could decipher anything, until
the patient's associations produced some insight. It came to her
mind that she had done some window-shopping the day before
the dream and seen a cape similar to the dream cape in the window
of one of the large department stores. But had she not seen many
other attractive things in her window-shopping tour? What had
made her choose the cape for dream material? It turned out that
this cape had struck her fancy because it had been worn by a
famous opera star and was on exhibit for the public. Oh, well,
somebody may say, the patient had ambitions to be an opera star
and borrowed this beautiful garment for her dream. But this patient had never had such ambitions, and this was not the reason
why she chose the cape of all the things on display in this window,
such as gloves, shoes, wig, and robe.

For the moment there were no further associations about the
choice of the cape, and neither analyst nor patient was the wiser.
By continuing to associate "freely"—that is, without seeming logic
or order—the patient added one detail to the dream, which she
had forgotten: "There was something exciting about you putting
the cape around my shoulders." What came to her mind with this

new detail? Nothing, at first; then the memory that she had gone window-shopping to look for a suit. She had not found anything she liked, and in the evening her father, who was a tailor, had offered to make a suit for her. She had agreed, and he had taken her measurements. Asked to go into detail about taking the measurements, it turned out that, at one point, her father stood behind her with the tape measure and measured the width of her shoulders, touching each shoulder with one hand—exactly as the analyst had done in the dream as he handed her the still mysterious cape. The excitement about being touched appeared to be related to an experience with her father the night before the dream. In the dream, it was the analyst who touched her. Why was the analyst substituted for her father? Had there been feelings about her father, exciting feelings, which she could not admit to herself? There had indeed been exciting and erotic feelings for her father, but they had existed more than a quarter of a century ago, when she had been five years old. These feelings had come to the surface of her conscious mind in previous sessions and should have been fully conscious by now. Why was it necessary to cover these feelings up again and use the analyst as a substitute?

A new association, based on a very old memory, began to clarify this question, as well as the choice of the cape. What came to mind now was an aunt whom the patient had not thought of for twenty years, an aunt who had long since died. At first, it was not very clear what this aunt was suddenly doing in her memory, but then an apartment house came into view and an elevator. She had gone down in the elevator with this aunt and something had happened. The old memory came to the surface: the patient had worn a rain cape in this elevator, a cape that was too long and that had caught in the sliding elevator door, frightening her because the hook at the neck of the cape had tightened around her. The aunt had quickly yanked the cape off, and the elevator had opened, freeing the cape. This incident now seemed very vivid and important. Why was it remembered and what did it have to do with the dream cape?

The aunt was the wife of the father's younger brother, a "ladies' man" who had always played around with other women and who had taken the patient on long car rides and seduced her into sexual play. She had been extremely guilty about these excursions and had never been able to look her aunt in the eye. Whenever she had been with her aunt, she had felt guilty. When the incident with the rain cape occurred, the patient had become panicky, as though this was a punishment, and when her aunt pulled off the cape, the patient had felt, "My aunt saved my life."

It was now becoming clearer why the patient had unconsciously selected the cape from all the articles in the window. The completely forgotten memory of the rain-cape-elevator episode had triggered off the interest in the spectacular cape, because to her a cape had a very spectacular meaning. This was becoming clearer only now, as she associated to the short dream. It had been her father's brother who had seduced her into sexual play, but from her associations to her father, who had taken her measurements, it appeared that her sexual feelings had been for her father and were displaced to the analyst in the dream. The feeling of excitement that she had dreamed and at first "forgotten" was a repressed memory that belonged to a very early sexual feeling for her father. Her uncle had been a substitute for her father in her fifth year, just as the analyst now was the substitute in her dream. The choice of the cape was significant for the re-experiencing of her forgotten guilt about "the other woman," who had originally been her mother.

Why was this material now used by the unconscious? What was the significance of all this at the present time in her life?

One of this patient's real problems was her inability to stand up for herself with other women, employers, wives of friends, and particularly older women. Her shyness and submissiveness with women bosses had prevented her from advancing in her field of work, and on the day of the dream she had had another tortuous experience with her boss, an older woman who had spoken to her very severely for an oversight that had not been her responsibility. The patient had been unable to tell her employer that she had had nothing to do with the mistake. Her unconscious guilt had prevented her from taking a realistic stand.

The dream began to throw some light on the sources of this unconscious guilt. A very short dream, which became meaningful in her analysis through her associations, of which we have seen a small aspect in part of one session.

Because dreams are often so very interesting and colorful, many patients become intrigued by the dream story and—to use a novelist's concept—forget about the plot. The difference, which is significant, was once defined by the novelist E. M. Forster. "The story is: 'The Queen died.' The plot is: 'The Queen died of grief.'" In analysis, the patient is more interested in the story, the analyst in the plot. The patient is satisfied with reporting what "happened," but the analyst is interested in the ways in which the story was arranged by the unconscious and in the needs that were met by the dream events. The only way to get at these is through the process of free association.

Patients often like to treat their own dreams as though they were movies, and quite frequently—and for good reasons—forget that in this "movie" they themselves were author and director, actor and cameraman, participant and audience. Having told their dream story, they would like to sit back and have the analyst tell them "what the dream means," as though he had the unabridged version of a dream book on his desk and had only to leaf through it to come up with the correct interpretation.

The general misconceptions about dream interpretation have a great deal to do with this attitude on the patient's part, but beyond this his attitude reflects a more significant lack on his part—his underlying unawareness of his own distinct identity. He has not yet discovered, deep down in his psyche, that he is an individual whose feelings cannot be exactly reproduced by any other individual. Like his fingerprints, his feelings may look similar to other people's feelings on superficial observation, but they cannot be duplicated.

It is a curious thing that most people know that the arrangement of lines on their thumb is completely distinct and differentiates them from all other people—but they make no such assumption about profound emotions like love and hate, jealousy and passion, sexual feelings and love of life. The tacit assumption is that "sexual" means more or less the same thing to everybody, and that "love" is experienced in the same way by all people.

To clarify this point, let us take one element that frequently plays an important part in dreams—the use of symbols. Without making any attempt to discuss the complex language of symbolic thinking, we can select at random a commonly accepted symbol. Most people would agree that the flag is a symbol of the country. While it is in reality a piece of cloth decorated with certain colors or insignia, it has come to represent a country, and it is treated as if it were more than a piece of cloth. It is revered, saluted, honored, because its symbolic meaning has been universally accepted. This does not, however, tell us anything about what the flag may mean to a certain individual. The flag, we have said, represents the country. But "country" is a vast concept encompassing the lives and feelings of many hundreds of millions of people. To each one of them, "country" represents something else: to one, the main street in a small New England town and the general store opposite the Methodist Church; to another, a skyscraper of glass and steel and the card game on the five-thirty commuter train; to still another, a supermarket on a Saturday afternoon with shopping carts lined up by the check-out counter; and so on. To some, it means the right to speak one's mind; to others, fear of old-age poverty. The word "country" may mean primarily a market place of ideas, or a melting pot of all existing cultures; an economic way of life, or a decaying civilization. The meanings are virtually unlimited, but they are not the same for any two people. The emphasis will differ, the feelings will differ—but all will agree that a flag symbolizes a country.

What could an analyst say if a patient used the symbol of the flag in his dream and expected the analyst to tell him the meaning, except that the flag symbolizes "country"? But if the patient continues to associate without censorship, his own very individual feelings about "country" will emerge. These feelings —conscious and unconscious—are inside his psyche, not in a dream book or in the psyche of the analyst. Even if the patient were very sophisticated and had accepted the intellectual equation of "country" with "parent," as expressed in such common phrases as "fatherland," "mother earth," "Uncle Sam," and so on, all that would help in his analysis would be his realization of his own complex feelings about father or uncle, mother or home. The universal meaning of the symbol would not go beyond the intellectual awareness he had had before he started analysis.

It is the same with all symbols. Only as the patient's very personal feelings—conscious and unconscious—emerge does the symbol take on personal significance. Neither patient nor analyst can know in advance what the unconscious meanings will be. Free association gradually reveals these meanings, and it is then that the analyst can help with the interpretations. Whether the patient reports a dream or talks about the weather, whether he shares some deep philosophical thought or complains about the traffic, whatever comes to mind is important and is treated with the same compassionate neutrality. Throughout the analysis, free association is the method of communication between patient and analyst.

THREE

·

The Patient-Analyst Relationship

The patient-analyst relationship, like the concept of psychoanalysis, cannot be understood in terms of a simple definition. To say, for example, that repressed or partially conscious feelings from the past are carried over (or transferred) from a figure in the past to the person of the analyst does not help in clarifying the nature of the relationship. Rather, it tends to oversimplify a complicated concept with which Freud and others wrestled for half a century and that continues to puzzle theoreticians and practitioners up to the present moment.

This particular relationship is at once personal and impersonal, dependent and independent, infantile and mature, with increasing frankness and revelation of the most hidden feelings on the one side and, to all intents and purposes, anonymity on the other. In no other human relationship does a person experience so much closeness and loneliness in one hour, cover such a wide range of emotions and ideas, race so quickly from past to present and back to the past—with no more action than the moving of the lips while lying quietly on a couch or sitting on a chair in a pleasant office.

It is a unique relationship. It is not a friendship or a teacher-student relationship; it is not the distantly friendly and somewhat impersonal relationship one has with a physician or a dentist. It is quite unlike the relationships one has with relatives or family, lovers or marriage partners, employers or colleagues. Like the whole process of psychoanalysis, it has to be experienced before it can be understood.

Perhaps it cannot even be called a "relationship," since the patient does not actually relate to the analyst as to another fellow human being. The patient uses the image of the analyst as a screen upon which to project images from his past life. This process makes it possible for him to re-experience. The less he faces the analyst, the less he knows about him, the more easily he can use him for the purpose of analysis.

Nor does the analyst, on his part, relate to the patient as he does to a friend—hence analysts cannot take on friends as patients —but structures the interaction to provide the best stage for re-enactment of the little and big tragedies of the patient's early years. He is constantly alert to what the patient says, and, more significantly, to how he says it, for the language of free association itself provides valuable leads into the hidden caverns of the unconscious.

Another unusual aspect of the relationship is the nature of privacy in analysis. While the analyst is absolutely committed to complete privacy and cannot discuss the content of any session with anybody else, the patient is of course free to discuss what he wishes and in whatever way suits him at the moment. The wife of a man in analysis could not hope to get any information from the analyst, but the husband himself may or may not share parts of his sessions with his wife. The same is true for any patient, whether he is an adult or a child, although in the analysis of young children, parents are sometimes more involved, as we shall see in the chapter on children. The analyst may suggest that the patient save all his thoughts for the analytic hour, instead of discussing them with others, but the patient may not always be able to accept such suggestions.

Certainly the patient wants to co-operate with the analyst; he pays for the doctor's time and he wants to get well as soon as possible. At the same time, he finds himself censoring some associations, fighting with the analyst, leaving out some unpleasant memories and actions from the day or the month before. One might say that he is not very reasonable if he opposes the very therapy he wants. But he is a patient, in the first place, precisely because there are, besides the reasonable, unreasonable forces inside his psyche that interfered so much with his self-interest that he sought analytic help. He did not plan to get sick; he always had the best intentions in his actions; but apparently the best intentions were not strong enough to cope with the irrational forces—early infantile drives, insufficiently channeled instincts, unconscious wishes that have remained active. It is the same unconscious forces that now militate against his getting well and are experienced as a constant fight against the analytic intervention.

Indeed, the patient's need to protect and repeat his old way of behaving, together with his awareness that this old way is really very bad for him, provide the live conflict that is re-enacted in the relationship with the analyst. Like an alcoholic who knows, when sober, the effect of his addiction but who is again and again flooded by his impulses, the analytic patient knows and does not know the effect when lifelong patterns of behavior come back to haunt him. Talking about some repetitious behavior to the analyst may produce feelings of guilt and make the analyst seem like a teacher who wags a finger at the naughty child. At other times, when the patient has been able to cope with a difficult situation in a less infantile way, he wants the analyst to shout "Bravo!" or expects some reward—again like a child.

If a patient finds it difficult to express a feeling or a fantasy, he may censor it and explain it to himself by saying, "This is not important." If the analyst intervenes at this point and inquires about the silence, the patient may see him as a nosy intruder, resent the question, and try to avoid the difficult issue. He reverts to the old foils he once employed to fool his parents or a friend, ducks out or changes the subject. If he succeeds with this maneuver in one session, he feels victorious and superior; he does not recognize that the seeming victory is in reality against his best interest. The infantile part of him has won, the mature part was defeated. Perhaps he will think of the analyst now as a friend, a nice guy who doesn't push and who is "understanding." Later that day, the more rational parts of his personality may assert themselves; he may remember that moment in the session and feel that the analyst is a dodo, somebody who can be fooled. The patient's emotions change and he despises the analyst. Sometimes feelings about the analyst go from intensive love to violent hate in one hour—depending on what emotions the patient experiences during the fifty minutes of analysis.

If we consider just the physical view for a moment, and think of the patient lying on the couch, we will realize that the analyst sees the back of his patient's head, while the patient sees the ceiling above. Although this is certainly not the most significant aspect of the relationship, so much has been said about the use of the couch—and it has been the basis of so many jokes—that perhaps we should explain just what its function is.

Historically, the use of the couch for therapeutic purposes is older than analysis. Dr. Josef Breuer, one of Freud's colleagues and early supporters, used it between 1880 and 1882 for inducing hypnosis in a now famous case of hysteria. The hypnosis resulted in the reproduction of hysterical symptoms in the doctor's office, and their subsequent disappearance. The patient termed this the "talking cure," and Breuer called it "catharsis," a then new method of psychotherapy. While he was developing the method of psychoanalysis, Freud continued to use the couch, at first to facilitate hypnosis, which he originally thought of as an essential step, later to facilitate recollecting, and still later for the process of free association. He also discovered that he could think about what his patients were saying, and understand them better if they did not search his face for answers to their troubles.

By now, there is ample evidence that many patients are aided in the process of re-experiencing through free association if they do not look at the analyst but use him to fill the many roles that were suggested in the previous chapter. Like all the analyst's interpretations, the use of the couch is aimed at facilitating the process of re-experiencing. It frees the patient to say anything that comes to his mind with less embarrassment than he would feel if he had to look at the analyst. It makes it easier for him to use the analyst as a sounding board or a "white sheet of paper" on which he writes his associations. And, finally, by reducing the sensitivity of his other senses, it helps the patient to talk, as it helps the analyst to listen.

There are also certain disadvantages. Since it is designed to help the patient discover his inner psychic mechanism, the couch also produces at times a feeling of isolation, the sensation that "I am talking to myself." This is not necessarily harmful, but for certain periods of the analysis, the negative aspects may outweigh the gains. Some analysts prefer a period of sitting up, prior to the use of the couch, as a sort of education for analysis. Other analysts use the couch with some patients and not with others. There is no question that the couch does encourage fantasies in some people and interferes with getting well. In such situations, as in the analysis of children, the use of the couch is not indicated.

The couch as a symbol of analysis is as insignificant as the white coat for the physician. Whether the patient looks at the wall or a face is not nearly so important as what he views inside himself. What matters is the discovery of the inner world of the individual, and it is this turbulent world that the analyst looks at throughout the whole process. He sees the untamed, primitive world of the unconscious, the most distorted reflections of his patient's fantasies, the expressions of early infantile wishes and anger, the sick preoccupation with the infantile self, the intensity of drives, and the overwhelming urges toward the discharge of hundreds of impulses. He listens to the patient's loneliness and hostility, struggles hour by hour with the patient's clinging to his inner tormentors, to his pain, his misery. He hears of wishes to die and to kill, to devour and to be devoured for safety, the torturous hunger for pain as the only way of experiencing the self. He hears his patient's wistful and melancholic cries for friends and a good world; he sees what life has done to the patient, and focuses more and more sharply on the nature of the fractures, on the hidden strength, the patient's wish to live and to create pleasure instead of pain for himself.

The picture the analyst has of the patient is far from objective; it is a clinical view. I once had to change an appointment and called a patient at her office. To my surprise, the voice on the other end was not the sad, pleading little voice I had heard for some time, but that of an energetic young woman who inquired smartly and with determination who was calling.

I should not have been surprised, because the patient had told me in the beginning that she was a young business executive, successful in her work. Shortly after that, however, the material that came from her was not about her career but about her unsuccessful relationships with people, both men and women. In many ways, she was emotionally retarded, as some people are mentally retarded. Certain aspects of her mind had overdeveloped for reasons that became slowly clearer as the analysis progressed; other aspects of her personality, indeed her entire emotional growth, remained on a primitive, early level.

I knew that she had considerable abilities and much strength in certain defined areas of her personality. This realistic fact was filed away in the back of my mind, just as her address and telephone number were filed away in my office. The fact by itself was no longer significant as the analysis went on; instead, the ways in which the compensation had developed became meaningful. When, for example, she described an important business deal in one of her associations, I was much more interested in her repetitious fantasies about the buyer than in the fact that she had saved her firm thousands of dollars. In her fantasy was hidden a part of the neurotic core that was significantly related to a certain distorted image she had of herself. I was interested in the fact that success meant very little to her.

Some patients screen out the healthy, rational aspects of their personality during the analytic hour because of their deep need to be taken care of and to appear incapacitated. Sometimes these aspects appear through slips of the tongue or other inadvertent associations. Other patients are so conditioned to a certain kind of behavior that they must picture themselves and their families as happy and successful, eliminating any material that would show the other side of the picture. These obvious extremes merely emphasize the fact that distortions continue to play a part in the patient-analyst relationship throughout the analysis. In practice, the distortions are very subtle and not at all obvious, but they are significant in describing the relationship between patient and analyst.

By definition, the patient does not have an objective picture of the analyst. Indeed, his realistic knowledge of the analyst may be compared to my knowledge of the young woman's telephone number and her position as a business executive. Just as I filed away this fact and concentrated on the business at hand—the treatment of the neurosis—so the young woman filed away in the back of her mind certain realistic facts about her analyst: his looks; his professional background and training; the fact that he understands French; his taste in furnishing an office; and perhaps some facts about his family she had learned from hearsay or gossip. All this became insignificant as she began to associate and to expose distortions and fantasies. As every analysis progresses, it matters less and less what the analyst is in reality, and more and more that he become useful to the patient for re-experiencing.

But, one may ask, doesn't this situation encourage fantasies and distortions? Doesn't the situation in which one person tells all and the other nothing make for an inequality comparable to early childhood, where only the child's needs matter? Isn't this situation conducive to making the patient more neurotic?

These are common and understandable questions, and they point the way toward an understanding of psychoanalysis, for they can all be answered in the affirmative. The relationship—from the analyst's point of view—is structured to encourage the expression of fantasies and distortions. The analyst does not put the distortions in his patient's mind; they were there to start with. But until they are expressed, openly, they cannot be seen, studied, understood, and worked out. The distortion in thinking—to use one common symptom of neurosis—has to be exposed to be treated, just as much as a growth in the lungs or a wound in the back. When patients say they feel exposed or undressed, they are describing symbolically what they are experiencing mentally. What is true for distortions in perceptions—overreactions, feelings that people are against you, slightly inaccurate memory—is also true for fantasies. Many of us know when we are having a fantasy: wouldn't it be nice to stay in bed this morning and take the day off? Commonly called daydreams or pipe dreams, these conscious fantasies don't present a problem because we usually recognize them at once as playful excursions of our fanciful mind and give them up after a short struggle. We shift gears, make contact with reality, know what we have to do, and do it, even though grudgingly at times.

Neurotic fantasies are more complicated and have to be uncovered via the relationship with the analyst before they can be seen by the patient. The patient is not aware that he is, in fact, fantasying. He has covered his daydreams with several layers of intellectual and often very brilliant explanations to make them inaccessible to rational observation.

The difference between fantasies that are conscious and those that are not is very apparent in childhood. The child knows that the piece of wood is not a wonderful boat, but he makes believe that it is; he wants to think it, and as long as he plays, he pretends that this is the most wonderful boat in the world. But his equally unreal fantasies about the power of his parents are the kind of fantasies that he does not recognize as fantasies. We call them illusions and hope that in time he can afford to become more realistic about his parents' limitations and weaknesses. While he is small, he is firmly convinced that his father can do whatever he wants; is very, very tall; and can get the child whatever he wishes. Although he is willing to give up the fantasy about the boat, he may not be ready to let go of the fantasy of parental omnipotence. He may need this illusion for a variety of reasons, and in spite of many sound and clear explanations, to which he nods solemn agreement, the fantasy about father or mother may be tucked away in a far corner of his mind to go on living—sometimes forever. Later in life he will talk as realistically as anybody else, but the early fantasies are still operating inside of his mind and will come out in many ways.

There are a great many categories of fantasies, of course, and, within the groupings, many levels, developed at different periods of infancy and early childhood. The causes for their development differ accordingly, but we may say that fantasies, generally, are substitutes for reality. Any satisfaction can be obtained through fantasy, through the process of imagination, through blurring the boundaries between what is real and what is not. A child may have discovered that he cannot get everything he wants. This realization does not come easily. It is one of the normal frustrations of growing up. While one part of his mind accepts this limitation, another part holds on to the idea that he can have or do whatever he wants. This second, illusory part may be kept alive by investing the imaginary power in another person, perhaps his older, stronger brother. This brother then becomes the symbol of unlimited power and ability, of omnipotence. By affiliating himself closely to his brother, he can keep his magical resource near him. But the realistic part of himself will not be content with this fantastic arrangement. It will seem to him, after a while, because the original fantasies are no longer conscious, that the brother really is so powerful, and he will resent the brother for it. So it will happen that the child both adores and resents his brother, his parents, and other important figures in his life. It is like lending a friend a valuable tool, forgetting that we have lent it, and then envying him for having it.

If somebody uses this mechanism of fantasying with many people, he will, after a time, forget that it was he who gave the others such powers, and instead experience envy and helplessness. "The others have all the luck," he will say. "I'm just no good." For many reasons, he may have to keep these early fantasies protected against reality and prove in his daily behavior that he is no good. Much of his behavior may be a defense of his early fantasies, and he will not let go of them easily in his relationship with the analyst. The battle will be continuous, and can be won only if the patient can experience once more—and this time with full awareness—what originally had made it necessary to cling to these fantasies. For this purpose, he will have to retrace his steps, travel back to the point in his life where the needs for the fantasies become visible and can be observed with the rational part of his mind. He may re-create the early illusions about his mother or father and feel once again small, attributing to the analyst the powers he once attributed to his parents. As he free-associates, as he relates dreams, the reasons for needing to cling to these fantasies will become apparent and the analyst can help him see them with new eyes, aiding him to re-evaluate what happened and to separate past from present.

It is therefore helpful if the patient's picture of the analyst is vague, and it is quite true that this picture encourages regression. But regression is one condition of re-experiencing, and it is the hub of the psychoanalytic method of treatment. The neurosis will unfold in the analytic relationship—instead of with the patient's family and business associates. The situation is structured to achieve this end, and from this fact stem a number of common confusions.

There are fantasies about falling in love with the analyst, becoming totally dependent on him, or changing religion, occupation, partners, social status, ideas, and philosophies as a result of the relationship with him. This relationship, frequently confused with a technical concept known as "transference," is supposed to represent some magical device by which the knowing analyst lures the unsuspecting patient into his trap, not unlike a witch doctor in the jungle of faith cure. There are other fantasies about the analyst as a bearded fool who listens or doesn't listen but who, in any case, has to sit somewhere near the reclining patient and write down every word the patient utters. In such fantasies, the analyst is a cold, detached observer who performs some kind of mental autopsy, taking a slice of this instinct and a sample of that ego derivative and storing them away in the refrigerator of his mighty mind, to be taken out at some future date.

These fantasies are very understandable because the patient-analyst relationship has more distortions than the other relationships a patient has in his lifetime. When he tells friends and relatives about it, they do not really understand, and they try to see it as similar to other human interactions they have known. Or, because they do not understand it, they may make fun of it, or use their imagination as a substitute for direct experience.

The patient sometimes becomes a carrier of the confusion as he reports aspects of his analysis, out of context, or as he acts out some aspects of it with friends or family. If a patient, for example, has reported in his analysis, over a period of sessions, how he feels continuously frustrated by everybody, how he expects more from people than he is getting, the analyst may ask for some concrete illustrations of this problem. The question itself irritates the patient because he feels the analyst should know what he means without demanding explanations. The analyst is not giving enough; he, too, is a source of frustration.

In spite of the irritation, the patient managed to recall some specific illustrations: Last night he read a chapter of his new novel to two old friends and their response was lukewarm—not that they didn't like it but they were not particularly interested in hearing anything in the first place; they just wanted to talk and have a drink. Other illustrations were the way his wife cooked. He had asked her time and again to let him do the shopping; he knew more about cuts of meat, but she insisted on feeling guilty if he did anything around the house, and would shop herself. The fact that his mother appeared every Friday night with a fried chicken, although she knew that he hated it; that his colleague in the office insisted on keeping the window open, in spite of his repeated demands to have it closed during cold days—he reported a continuous row of little frustrations. Nobody understood him. When the analyst suggested that the patient had difficulty making compromises, the patient was silent for several minutes. What went on during these few minutes was not verbalized until the next session; between the two sessions the patient's anger remained inside him and was directed at people outside the analytic office. He left the session and cursed the analyst under his breath. When his wife asked him whether he had had a good session, the patient got furious. "Good session?" he shouted. "That bastard of an analyst called me a tightwad, insinuated that I can't share with people and want everything my way." When his wife did not reassure him—because she felt that way about him herself—he became angrier at his wife. "Well?" he demanded. "Say something. Tell me that it's not true, that I'm not a cranky old fool! Are you calling me selfish, too?"

The wife, of course, had no idea what had brought all this on, but she deduced that the analysis was making her husband even more difficult. "I don't know," she might muse to her friends. "Analysis is certainly not making my husband any easier to live with. Sometimes I think he was better off before he started the whole damn thing." It would not be surprising if after this her friends went away with the idea that analysis is a dubious undertaking at best.

In a complicated marital situation, a young wife in analysis sounded as if she were the victim of an insensitive villain to whom she seemed chained. It soon appeared in her free associations that she had had this image of herself more or less through life. She was not at all aware of the other side of it—that she had often had her own way in childhood and in her marriage by appearing submissive. While actually by playing the martyr and making others feel sorry for her, she was able to do what she wanted. When, at one point in her therapy, the analyst wondered whether she had no choice over her actions, the patient took this to mean that she should do exactly what she felt like at any given moment. She went home after her analytic hour, did not make supper, and left her husband a note saying she was going out for the evening. She explained that her analyst had "told" her to make her own choices over her actions and this was what she was going to do. If he did not like her the way she was, he could leave. The husband, unfamiliar with psychoanalysis, got furious at the analyst, felt protective of his poor, misguided wife, and played unknowingly into her victim role. When the patient came to her next analytic hour, she reported her husband's rage, the fuss he had made because for once she had not felt like preparing supper, and then got angry at her analyst, from whom she expected more sympathy and support in her misery. She got even angrier when her analyst pointed out that he had not "advised" her to do anything at all, but had asked her in the previous hour whether she seemed to have no choice over her behavior. She burst into tears and felt, she said, betrayed and deserted. At this point, she was re-experiencing a situation from her childhood in which she had repeatedly played her mother against her father by declaring herself helpless in such a way that her father was moved by her tears and took her side against his wife. She discovered later in her analysis that she had formed a habit of playing two authority figures against each other in order to have her way—usually by appearing as the innocent bystander, the victim to whom things always "happened." As she repeated this behavior now in the analytic hour, she had a new experience—there was no reaction to her tears. There was no approval, no disapproval—the analyst did not act like mother or father. Her old behavior did not work. She left this session in a state of fury, but two sessions later reported a dream that revealed her unconscious awareness of her victim role. Apparently the experience in the analytic session had had some effect on the unconscious layers that had hidden her domination-through-suffering from her own consciousness.

Although this vignette is greatly oversimplified and does not contain any important data from the patient's unconscious, it may illustrate the problem of behavior outside the analytic hour and the way in which some patients use the analytic relationship in dealing with friends and family. This aspect will be discussed in a later chapter.

It also illustrates one of the ways in which some patients contribute to the general confusion about analysis. If this patient's husband had not been a rather reasonable man, he might well have stormed out of the house and told his friends that the crazy analyst was trying to break up his home. If he had had the slightest delusion of persecution, he might have used this episode to fantasy about the analyst's designs on his pretty wife. And his friends, in turn, would form an opinion about psychoanalysis from his story.

If one remembers that most opinions about analysis are formed on such a basis, it is easy to see why there is such confusion. General knowledge about psychoanalysis comes mostly from patients who have been analyzed or from people who are in analysis.

People who have successfully completed an analysis learned somewhere along the line that the less they chatted or gossiped about the process, the more they succeeded in using the analyst for re-experiencing and getting well by slowly working through their problems. They do not talk much about analysis, except to indicate that they feel the experience has been helpful to them. Patients who have had an unsuccessful analysis are much more likely to talk about it, because they naturally prefer to blame the method or the practitioner rather than themselves. They are frustrated, unsatisfied with analysis for many reasons, and unlikely to be particularly objective about the experience.

Patients in analysis cannot be expected to have much perspective about an experience that involves them so deeply. Since the unconscious, irrational aspects of their psyches are prominent in the process, their rational judgment about the treatment and the analyst has to be distorted. The reports on individual analytic sessions, or about the analyst—whether positive or negative, or both, at different times—should not be taken at face value. At times the patient will like the analyst, at other times hate him, and at other times consider him simply a friendly person who does not change.

This is characteristic of both the patient-analyst relationship and the treatment method. Only as the analyst remains steady and unaffected by the patient's associations can the patient change. This is a continuous source of frustration throughout the whole process—indeed, it is synonymous with it. The natural desire of everyone is to keep the status quo and have the other fellow make the adjustment. The patient, as he re-experiences drives and wishes from early childhood, is using both childhood methods and a mature intellect to get the analyst to comply with his wishes and drives, and to change, so that he, the patient, can remain as he is. This may sound contradictory, since the patient entered treatment in order to change, but this desire cannot be very powerful, or the neurosis would not have developed in the first place. Somewhere along the line, some infantile desires gained the upper hand with the patient's personality and affected his thinking, feeling, action. It is understood that the patient clings to the neurosis in spite of his being in analysis, and this explains why patients sometimes find analysis disappointing and frustrating, especially in its early phases.

This is easier to understand if one thinks of the difficulty anybody has in trying to change deeply ingrained, long-standing habits. Once we have made an adaptation, we are usually loath even to consider modification—although we recognize with our intellect that these changes may be "for our own good." We do not have to think of such deeply anchored adaptations as attitudes or ways of thinking; we need only recall such common problems as giving up smoking or trying to diet. Anybody who is aware of his prejudices knows what a steep, uphill battle he will have once he disapproves of his prejudice and yet remains emotionally tied to it. A man with a deep-seated prejudice against Negroes, for example, who has recognized that his attitude is irrational, usually has a lifetime battle with his prejudice, which has deep and old roots. Such a man knows well the conflict between feeling and thinking.

The changes that occur in analysis require more intensive work because, until he begins analysis, the patient has not even been conscious of the fact that many of his thoughts and feelings have an irrational, unconscious, or infantile basis. The man who has recognized that there is something wrong with his social attitudes is at least aware of a conflict and of the need for change. The patient in analysis feels miserable or out of step with the world or troubled in some way, but he doesn't know as yet that, without meaning to, he has made a faulty adjustment to reality and will first have to discover it and then proceed to change it.

One patient, for example, adapted to reality by locking up all his normal, aggressive impulses and trying to be loved and respected through being extremely submissive and polite to everybody. He could not understand why people were not nice to him:

Wasn't he polite and obliging; didn't he help his fellow man whenever he could; wasn't he the most unselfish of persons?

This basic attitude was visible in all his thinking, feeling, and actions. It became visible in the very beginning of his analysis, when he arrived for his second appointment and did not ring the bell but sat quietly in the waiting room. When his analyst inquired about it—since he had told the patient the previous time to ring the bell and come in—the patient replied in characteristic fashion: "I did not want to disturb you or the other patient."

When the analyst took this up and wondered whether it was merely a matter of good manners, the patient got very annoyed. What did the analyst want from him? Did he want him to become inconsiderate? He said that he took pride in being thoughtful and helpful, and he most certainly had no intention of changing.

In contrast to the man who knew that racial prejudices are irrational, this patient had not yet come to the point where he could realize the need for change. He had come to analysis because he was unhappy in his work, had noticed homosexual tendencies in himself, and could not make any decisions at all. He had imagined, he said later, that the analyst would give him some advice, some suggestions, something like medicine to make him feel better. He had never thought of analysis as a process of inner metamorphosis, and for the entire first year of his analysis he resented the idea of hard work and change. He felt it was enough that he came and paid money; did he also have to talk and, especially, talk about things that were so disagreeable?

Understandably, this patient's relationship with his analyst went through many phases and had to change constantly as his early feelings became visible and were re-experienced. He verbalized the common conflict very openly when he inquired why he, the patient, had to make all the adjustments and changes. Why was the analyst so rigid and inflexible and unwilling to change one bit? How was he, the patient, going to learn if the analyst did not show him how to do it better? Was this relationship not a give-and-take proposition, like all other relationships? Gradually, it seemed to the patient that his analyst was not very different from his father, whom he had hated all his life. As he recounted the many unjust things his father had done to him—in reality not very different from the behavior of many fathers—the analyst inquired into details of these standard complaints. Every inquiry seemed to the patient like a hostile criticism of himself, a defense of his father. He asked, "Whose side are you on, anyway?"

When he had run out of the few unpleasant memories that had a reality basis, he began to have his first doubts about the deeper reasons for his hostility toward his father. He had to recognize that while all he had said was true, it was not really a sound explanation for a very deep and long-standing hate. The feelings remained, but his thinking began to change. This was a very slow process, with continuous resentment against the analyst, who was to him what his father had seemed to be in childhood. Every question was received as a scolding or a punishment: "I am always wrong, no matter what I say. I hate you for this."

The resemblances between father and analyst seemed to increase until the two images merged into one: the patient felt that he was a small boy talking to his father. It occurred to him that he wanted the analyst's approval and respect—indeed, he wanted his love, something he had not had from his father. Fantasies kept coming to mind in which he would be close to his analyst, sit close to him, feel his presence. There were thinly disguised homosexual dreams that frightened him until he discovered that it was safe to report these dreams, since the analyst remained where he was—quietly in his chair, changing neither position nor attitude. Much later, it became clear that the patient from his earliest infancy had been used by his mother as her confidant and was made to listen to all her bitter feelings against her husband. Her deep hatred of men, particularly of her husband, was absorbed by the patient long before he had a chance to make up his own mind about his father, and men in general. He actually hated men before he even knew that he was a male himself. Masculinity was a dirty word in his mind. He had identified with his mother during his formative years and had wished he could have been a woman. Since he could not change his sex, he did the nearest thing to it— he felt and acted like his mother in every possible way. Like her, he became submissive and polite; like her, he never spoke honestly to his father, locking up his hate for him, as she had done. He avoided taking a stand on any question, remained diffident and uncertain, withdrawing from all close contact with boys and becoming terrified of girls, who, he said, expected him to act like a man. He happened to be very good-looking, by common standards, and had an exceptionally good mind. He had developed none of his possibilities, and sounded dull and suspicious to most people.

As he used the relationship with the analyst to discover that his aggressive wishes were not dangerous, it appeared to him that other people were changing. Suddenly, and without apparent reason, they seemed to be much nicer to him. A co-worker offered him a ride home in his new car. A girl who worked on the same floor smiled at him, and when he spoke to her, she responded in a warm and friendly way. His employer offered him a chance for advancement, involving more responsibility and more money. Among the people who seemed to be changing was his analyst. The patient said he was surprised to find his analyst so interested in him all of a sudden. If he had seemed like father on occasion, the analyst now appeared more like his servile and doting mother.

The same "Come in, please," that he had heard many times before from his analyst no longer sounded like a forbidding, threatening call but like a warm, kind welcome. Where previously the same phrase had been experienced as a signal to danger, it now led to a fantasy of being invited into a house, as a guest for dinner. It was his mother who had served him dinner every day of his life until the present time, and he had never wondered about it until now. The idea of a home of his own was a new experience in thinking.

Because new experiences are by definition unfamiliar, this patient, like many other patients, tried to avoid the full impact of his. He did this by assuming that the analyst was changing, not himself. For a time, he was quite sure that the analyst greeted him in different ways, felt differently about him, had changed his opinions and attitudes.

Like a passenger sitting in a moving train that passes another train standing in a station, the patient cannot be sure whether he is moving and changing or whether it is the other object. The confusion between oneself and the other fellow is worked through in the relationship with the analyst. Only as the analyst remains constant can the patient become aware of his own self and the objective reality outside of himself. The relationship enables him to distinguish between the inside of himself and the outside world, between his powerful drives and wishes and the outside world, which does not bend to his demands. Only through the compassionate neutrality of the analyst can the patient experience reality and his own limitations. Once this awareness is clear and strong, the analyst will no longer seem to have magical powers, nor will he seem cold and detached. He will not be needed any more as a screen on which to project mental images from the past; there will be no more curiosity about the analyst and his life; fantasies will no longer be necessary. The relationship will serve no further purpose: the analysis is completed.

FOUR

·

The Patient in Analysis

Many people who are thinking about undergoing analysis expect to find in the process some kind of soul-searching, deep introspection, and talk about basic problems and ideas. In their minds, analysis is similar to archaeology, and the verb most frequently associated with it is "digging." They are usually looking forward with trepidation or excited anticipation to "finding myself," to learning about the cause of their troubles and understanding how to be "better human beings."

For these reasons, they are often disappointed when their analyst asks them to talk off the top of the head, and suggests that they say whatever comes to the surface of their mind. There is the common feeling of being superficial, of talking about nothing very much and spending valuable time and hard-earned money discussing banalities and trifles. This process seems a far cry from the exciting discovery of "insights" they had hoped for.

Usually the idea of insight is based on the earliest learning experiences, in which a parent tells a child what it wants to know. Just as a small child expects its parent, quite naturally, to provide the answers to all questions, the patient assumes that the analyst somehow knows what is really unknown. When he asks, often in exasperation, "Why am I acting like this, what makes me cause so much pain to people I love, why do I repeat the same nonsense for years and years?" he hopes to get an answer from the oracle-analyst and is vaguely convinced that the analyst really knows but won't tell him, because of some theory according to which the patient has to find out for himself. He frequently clings to the belief that if the analyst does not tell him the answers, it is because he does not want to, because the patient has been "bad," unco-operative, "resistant" or something else negative. It is very difficult for many patients to reconcile themselves to the fact that the analyst has no X ray with which to penetrate the unconscious mind, that only the emergence of free associations produces the material that makes unconscious mechanisms accessible to observation.

The whole idea of the "unconscious" does not have much reality for the patient until he has experienced the workings of this part of his psyche. That "unconscious" may be equated with "unknown" in the psyche usually does not have too much meaning for patients in the beginning of analysis. It is one thing to speak of a "subconscious" idea—which customarily means preconscious, and fairly near the surface of conscious knowledge—and quite another to fathom the idea that all of us are only partially aware of the reasons for our actions. Usually this partial, conscious awareness is enough for rational living; sometimes it is not. Usually we make no more contact with our unconscious mind than we make with our internal organs. We know we have a heart and kidneys, a liver and lungs, but this knowledge does not have much meaning as long as these organs function normally. We don't always know where they are located, how they function, what their purpose is—and we don't care, because there is no need to be aware of the existence of internal organs.

We also know there is a part of the brain known as the unconscious, but as long as it doesn't bother us, we are content to use it as a casual, playful part of ourselves, nice for parlor games, useful for discovering why we forgot something, fascinating for speculation about what made us do the very thing we didn't mean to do. But we don't actually understand the complicated system of the unconscious, and we don't yet acknowledge it as an extremely vital, central part of the brain. This is due in part to the fact that the scientific discovery of the unconscious is less than a century old.

From the earliest development of man to the present day, the mind has been extolled as the distinguishing mark of the human being. Human ingenuity, human supremacy over the world of animals, human power have come to be equated with superior mental abilities. From uncountable time, "mind" has meant consciousness. Mental life has been identified as consciousness; thinking and reasoning have been considered functions of the conscious mind. The discovery of a substratum of consciousness that proved to be of far greater significance to the human mind than consciousness was tremendously shocking to people, and it explains, in part, the hostility toward and fear of psychoanalysis. Although the records of mythology, of poetry, and of drama show very clearly that man has always needed to find explanations for human behavior outside the conscious mind, it is more comfortable to ascribe unexplainable behavior to superhuman causes than to challenge the age-old axiom that mind equals consciousness.

At this point of history, we have, in some parts of the world, a token acknowledgment of the existence of the unconscious. It is tolerated as a concept or else it is ignored, while the popular ideas of the mind have barely advanced beyond the witch-burning of the Middle Ages. You are either "normal" or you are "crazy"; you are "intelligent" or "stupid," as if Freud's discoveries had never been made—an apt illustration of man's reluctance to change, which is, after all, the purpose of the psychoanalytic treatment method.

It is understandable, then, that patients come to analysis with skepticism and doubt, and cannot contemplate the existence of the unknown part of the mind without some trepidation or fear. Even after we have conceded that there is more to the psyche than is conscious or meets the eye or any of the other senses, we hesitate, quite naturally, to follow a stranger on a journey into the hitherto unknown parts of the mind.

Sooner or later, this journey leads into the formidable labyrinth called memory, one of the most intricate mazes known to man. If we knew half as much about the interlocking systems in the elusive mechanism of the memory as we do about the atom, we could be more precise in our analytic explorations, our educational methods, our predictions of human behavior. Our ignorance about the learning process, our ability to remember and forget and remember again, our partial and screened memories, our distortions of past experiences—all are connected with our lack of more accurate knowledge of the labyrinth, memory.

The memory, imperfectly though we understand it, is one of the major theaters of analytic operation. When Freud suggested that the neurotic suffers from forgotten memories, he indicated one of the important mechanisms in analysis—the human ability to put certain perceptions or sensations so far back into the memory file that it cannot be found any more. We then believe that the memory is "lost," the event "forgotten," and that, in fact, the whole thing never happened. Short of this extreme mechanism, we usually misfile only parts of an experience, or distort it enough to make it acceptable to our conscious mind.

Patients discover that, in analysis, events that seemed to have been permanently misplaced in the memory return to consciousness. They discover or rediscover feelings or persons of whom they have not consciously thought for years. As the necessity for forgetting is removed, older feelings return. In dreams, people whom one may not have thought of for a quarter of a century or more begin to appear. Some memories return strongly and hide still more important events, which are forgotten—that is, not yet recalled. One patient, for example, had the greatest difficulty recalling experiences that made him feel constantly in mortal danger, as though he were a prisoner behind bars. After a very long time, he suddenly remembered a detail from early childhood—the vertical bars on his crib, which reminded him, in recollection, of prison bars. He was very much relieved when he produced this forgotten memory, and considered the fear removed. He dwelt for some time on the bars, the crib, the room, the ceiling, enjoying the long-repressed memory, which came back with more and more vividness.

What he did not recall at that time—but what emerged through dreams, months later—was the view from his crib: it had been the view of his parents' double bed and his observation of their sexual intercourse up to his fifth year. He had reacted to this with panic and considered his father a dangerous attacker whom he would have to be afraid of. Connected with this were a number of basic early feelings, which, however, all remained hidden behind the crib memory. The crib recall was like a screen behind which more important events were hidden. These so-called screen memories are admitted to consciousness after a time, while more important events remain hidden behind them, somewhat in the way that a gangster admits income-tax evasion but denies a gang killing.

The high selectivity of our memory, the many complex ways in which events of early infancy and childhood leave memory traces, like petrified footsteps; the ways in which we use the stored and the discarded memories to cope with our instincts and our self image; the screen memories—all are of great importance in the analytic process.

For example, there is the statement made by one patient, "If I can't remember something, it didn't happen." Taken at face value, such a statement makes no sense at all. Certainly the patient, a young woman of reasonable intelligence, knew that the Civil War had happened, even though she did not remember it. This, then, could not be what she had meant. Since all associations, whether rational or irrational, have meaning in the conscious or unconscious mind, her statement needed to be taken apart, or analyzed, to be understood. Since it had to do with memory, it was likely that the patient wished to deny some feelings or events from her own history that were, at the moment, not acceptable to her. By making the statement in this generalized fashion, she also wished to indicate that this was a general feeling, not related to anything specific. She was fighting the reality of some early events and feelings that she had managed to forget.

In the process of re-experiencing and with the evidence accumulated from a series of clear dreams, these early events and feelings were about to return to consciousness. One of the feelings that emerged was her intense hate for her older brother. The patient could not accept this feeling from the past, since she had formed the self-image of a loving and considerate sister. She had spent considerable time, energy, and money caring for her brother—indeed, she felt she had sacrificed part of her life for him. As far as her conscious mind was concerned—and this was all she knew—nobody could have been a better sister than she had been and, in fact, continued to be. Why, just that morning she had invited him to dinner, something that her husband did not appreciate, for it was to be a wedding-anniversary dinner. "I had to fight with my husband for this invitation. I could have saved myself a great deal of trouble if I were not considerate and loving to my brother—how can you say that I feel anything but love for him?"

When the analyst called to the patient's mind some associations from previous sessions, which also had revealed very mixed feelings about her brother, the patient used the memory as an armor, just as she had done through most of her life. She could not remember having said these things; perhaps the analyst was confused or had mixed her up with some other patient.

Much later, the deeper reason for her need to deny any kind of anger or hostility against her brother appeared—a strong early sexual attraction, which had been promoted by him. If she admitted to herself that she had had hostile feelings, she would then have to ask for the causes and would discover that she had hated him for his seductive attempts and his rejection of her after she responded. Once this was admitted, she would have to recall her part in these games and the stronger wishes behind her innocuous, childish actions, and her guilt would emerge full force. The guilt had been there all the time but was expressed in such self-sacrificing actions as she had described. This kind of release of guilt was more acceptable to her than facing her strong early sexual involvement. Still later, the connection between her repressed, incestuous wishes and her marital choice and marital conflicts became apparent. When she had reported the episode in which she had invited her brother to her wedding-anniversary dinner, there had been no conscious awareness of the deeper meaning of this action.

The meaning of her statement, "If I can't remember something, it did not happen," emerged in the light of subsequent analytic findings. At the time she made the statement, the analyst did not know the deeper meaning of it either. He could only wonder about the strength of her need to deny any kind of anger or even mildly disagreeable feelings toward her brother, and speculate that there might be an area of unresolved conflict. Only as the associations provided the material was the analyst able to put together some of the pieces of the puzzle and share this awareness with his patient.

Once there is enough material for the analyst to make a statement, the patient may or may not be ready to consider this new view of himself. But even after the rational part of the mind is ready to give up some of its defensive operations, the patient has a long way to go until the new findings are fully integrated into his total personality. In the last-cited case, the patient's recognition of strong incestuous wishes and some sexual child behavior was only the beginning of the cure. Many patients get ready to recognize new ideas about themselves while their emotional roots from the past remain untouched. The process of integrating the new ideas with more mature emotions is known as "working through" the conflicts, and represents the most significant part of the analysis.

People who have not had a full analysis, for one reason or another, are often heard to complain that they "know" what makes them act the way they do, but, that this has not stopped them from continuing to do so. The knowledge, as it were, has not been integrated, the "insight" has remained separate from the emotional roots. There has been no working through of inner conflicts.

What does this essential process really mean? Why is rational knowledge not sufficient?

The last mentioned patient may provide the answer. She made a statement, "If I don't remember something, it did not happen." This statement, which was made with some cynicism, some doubt, and half-jokingly—all indications of some awareness on the patient's part of her irrational nature—nevertheless represented one important aspect of her thinking mechanism.

It was made at a mature age, when she was a married woman, a mother, a successful businesswoman. This manner of thinking—which often led to corresponding action—could have been reflected in some other statements of hers. She could have revealed her way of dealing with reality in hundreds of different ways, but the mechanism of distorting or denying what she did not want to recognize would have come out in each one of them. For example, in her office, when an order she had written was returned, for one reason or another, she might insist that she had never written the order at all. (If I don't remember something, it didn't happen.) She would be called stubborn by her employees, perhaps, or strong-willed by her friends. Whatever form this aspect of her character took, it would always reveal the same formula: "If I don't remember something, it didn't happen." Before she could spot this tendency in herself, she would first have to see the many ways in which it was expressed—with her brother, her husband, her employees, her friends—and not until she realized that she was the common denominator in all these situations could she even begin fully to understand the range this thinking distortion encompassed. This is one part of the working-through process.

It requires sufficient free associations, reflecting many life situations, for the patient to see for himself how a certain kind of thinking is repeated. This is working through horizontally, in width or across a wide range of experiences. The other kind of working through is more complex because it is vertical, going into depth and connecting the past with the present.

When the patient made this statement—which was originally used to illustrate the mind-equals-consciousness fallacy and its link with memory—it was connected through her associations with her older brother. It turned out that since she could not accept her very early feelings about her brother, she had chosen to "forget" them; that is, to deny them. It is reasonable to assume that there were other early feelings that she had chosen to "forget" in the same or similar ways. By beginning with the same statement—or similar ones—and producing further associations, it was possible to get at other early roots of thinking disturbances or related character problems. Only when a patient can see the breadth and depth of his unconscious operating can an insight have live meaning. In other words, the patient mentioned might very well accept the idea that she had had all kinds of feelings about her brother that she had denied. However, this kind of awareness would not have much meaning for her, since it would be associated in her mind only with the one specific relationship to her brother, and, within this relationship, only to the one aspect described. She would not see this as a manner of dealing with conflicts in all areas of her life, nor would she be able to give up this mechanism without working through enough episodes in depth.

Many patients go through a good deal of torture trying to remember what happened in the analytic hour. Some people go so far as to keep notes, others try for total recall and attempt to play back the whole interchange on the way home or for the rest of the day. There are many reasons for this, but none of them is very sensible. The analyst's office is not a classroom, and the patient is not a student. While there are learning elements in any experience, the patient will not gain any more from the experience by keeping track of "how much I have learned today." On the contrary, the chalking up of intellectual knowledge, the weighing of the profit or loss of each session, the imaginary keeping watch over the process, are in reality all interferences with the working-through process. To keep track of the complexities of the psychic mechanism is the analyst's job; the patient's job is free association, a process that requires all his available energy, as we pointed out in the beginning.

The inner changes come about as gradually as the working-through process. There is no sudden flash of "insight," no brilliant intellectual illumination. The moments of "Oh, I see now," which are the first awareness before the working through, may be compared to the inspiration of a composer. While the motion pictures commonly portray a composer as a man who has an inspiration and then reels off the finished symphony, the reality of the working-through process is not shown, partially because it would be boring to watch. Actually, the creative process can be compared to the analytic process. The inspiration that produces the musical theme is comparable to the inspiration of "Now I see why I asked my brother to our wedding-anniversary dinner." But this does not produce a major character change, any more than the first bar of Beethoven's Fifth Symphony represents the total work of art. The theme is in the first bar, but what makes the symphony is the way in which the composer has worked with the theme, developed it, restated it, varied it—worked it through. This is the actual work that produces the result. The original insight springs from the creative unconscious; the "ninety per cent perspiration," which is the popular definition of genius, is the hard and slow process of working through.

The manner of working through, its speed or intensity, the reworking of basic themes, and the fighting off of the gradual recognition vary as much from patient to patient as the creative process or the learning process differs from individual to individual. No two people learn alike, no two people create alike, and no two patients in analysis work through their conflicts in exactly comparable ways.

This recognition highlights a basic axiom—generalizations about the analytic process are quite meaningless. But people ask what analysis is like, and they want some rough idea of the process. If they are told that this is very different for everybody, they get a little irritated because the answer is a truism. Every experience is different for each individual. Skiing may be like flying for me; it may be a heightened feeling of body control for you. One skier will be full of the beauty of the intense whiteness and the blue skies, another will see the long legs and small hips of young girls passing in front of him. Of course, every experience is felt differently by each one of us.

This is not the issue. The outside world is experienced differently by each of us. This is, of course, also true for the experience of analysis. But the major point is the fact that in the analytic experience the patient is both subject and object: I discover myself. There is no common denominator with other people, as in skiing or learning or being married. It is possible to compare one's own experience of skiing or being married with that of others. There is the individual as a subject, who refers to some object outside of himself—spouse, textbooks, teacher, nature. Although the subjects differ in their reactions, they at least have a common point of reference. Not so in analysis. In this experience, the individual as a subject observes, not the mountains, social issues, or a lover, but himself. To put it abstractly and in a very oversimplified way—in analysis, different parts of the personality are the issue. The rational, healthy parts are observing and coping with the irrational and unconscious parts of the personality. Each of these parts is unique for each individual. Within these parts there are more individual aspects—for example, the way I see myself or the way I want to be seen by others, the way I am and the way I would like to be. These are just a few segments of the rational part of the personality.

There are more numerous aspects to the irrational and unconscious parts. The continuous interplay of these overlapping and intertwined parts of the personality constitutes some of the analytic experience. Is it not clear why patients declare their inability to compare their analysis with that of anybody else? Could one possibly generalize about the experience of analysis?

Yet, some people will say, patients continue to make all kinds of comparisons of their experience. At first glance, this seems like a contradiction. Perhaps the puzzle can be solved by borrowing a very illuminating association from a patient who once said, "When I'm alone, there's nobody there." This had been a very free association, coming without censorship by the intellect and without regard to whether it made sense right away or not. The phrase had just come to her mind, and after she had said it, she smiled to herself and laughed, because on second thought it sounded amusing to her. Yet this association happened to reflect one of her most basic problems and that of many patients who, like her, experience the outside world not through their own senses but through somebody else. Her need to merge with somebody else—beginning in infancy with her mother—was so intense that she had developed a very keen intuition about other people, and very often could sense what a friend or a lover felt, whereupon she borrowed these feelings. Understandably, this patient one day remembered, as one of her associations, the joke about the two analysts, one of whom says to the other, "You are fine. How am I?" This was, however, no joke to this patient, because she could indeed tell how somebody else felt but did not know how she herself felt, because her own self-image was not well developed. This patient would ask other patients in her acquaintance about their analyses and then try to feel something about her own.

That this patient had to ask about the analytic experiences of her acquaintances was by itself a symptom of her insufficiently developed identity. For some patients, this is a casual inquiry or perhaps scientific curiosity. There are still other patients who find themselves talking about their analysis and trying to compare it with the analytic experiences of other patients because they are searching for a model, as though they were afraid to say everything that comes to mind in their own analysis without a stamp of approval from somebody who has done the same. These patients resemble the woman quoted above, who felt that when she was alone, there was nobody there. She, too, was making a lifelong search for models, and tried never to antagonize anybody because she felt that without an object she was nonexistent. Like many patients, she wanted to be the ideal patient, the most co-operative and successful patient.

Such common wishes echo the well-known fantasies of childhood—to be the favorite child, the best student, worker, lover, father, or mother. They seem to stay with some people throughout life, adapting themselves throughout the progressive age levels. It is not particularly surprising that they appear most forcefully in analysis. To be "the best"—to exist via comparison—is actually a substitute for self-realization, and represents a torturing frustration, comparable to the wish to catch one's own shadow.

The patient who felt there was nobody in the room when she was alone had in common with other patients the fantasy that she was most secure and protected when she was most unobtrusive. This was part of the "best"-child-and-patient illusion, and it was understandable that she did not like to say much, because this would not only make her very obtrusive but put her in the limelight. Since she had lived through her childhood with the fantasy that she would be safe from harm if she were perfectly still and quiet, talking, in itself, seemed dangerous at first. But since there was the desire to be co-operative and do what she was told, she overcame the hesitation to speak, and tried to associate. In line with her life development and character, she reported that everything was fine. She censored all complaints, feelings of discomfort, expressions of anger or hate.

It was less difficult for her to talk about the growing-up problems of her daughter. This gave her the feeling that "somebody is there when Julia is in the room." She had made herself indispensable in the life of her daughter and anticipated with fear the next few years, in which, she knew, young people break away from their parents. She had many interesting and profound things to say about mother-daughter relationships. She had equally pungent observations about her husband and close friends—but she never expressed her feelings about herself. This was, of course, to be expected, since she did not feel that she existed by herself, and thought she did not experience feelings of her own.

There were glimpses of personal expression at the beginning and end of the hour, associations that, for a time, she considered did not belong to the analytic process. These remarks seemed trivial to her, too banal even to express. She could not see what her offhand remarks about other patients she had met in the office had to do with her deep problems. She did not consider it the least bit significant that she delayed coming into the office at every session and hurried out at the end, always after having asked whether the hour was over. That she was expressing feelings with this behavior did not occur to her.

She could not admit to herself that she did not really want to be in analysis but that, as usual, she was doing what everybody had advised her to do and, now that she was coming, she was going to be a good girl and co-operate, come hell or high water. When the analyst assured her that everything she had to say was of interest in the analysis, she finally volunteered that the patient who came after her looked a little bit like her daughter.

Asked about the similarity, the patient said that the young lady was just as unfriendly as her daughter. She always said hello to her when she came out of the office, but the young patient never answered. This was like her daughter. The analyst wondered whether it might not be a little frustrating to greet somebody several times a week in the same place and never get a response. Oh, no, the patient said. She was used to this; at home, her daughter never answered her when she asked her a question, except when she felt like it.

When the analyst waited for more associations, the patient went on in defense of her daughter. This was the younger generation; one had to understand young people. When there was still no rejoinder from the analyst, the patient became anxious. Probably, she said, the analyst had no children or knew little about young people. The young patient who followed her must be the same kind of person as her daughter. She wondered how such a person could be a co-operative patient. If she were the analyst, it might not be easy for her to like such a person. Could she ask a personal question? Was it not true that the analyst expected co-operation from his patients? How then could he work with a person like this? The analyst suggested that the patient surely could understand this situation, since she seemed to have a similar problem at home.

There followed a prolonged silence, the first one in this patient's analysis. She allowed herself to be "unco-operative." The analyst waited and then suggested that the patient seemed to have had some thoughts that were hard to express. After another pause, the patient said, with feeling, that a horrible thought had just occurred to her, which she was trying to forget. Did this have to do with her daughter, the analyst asked. The patient nodded, and said, in a whisper, the idea had occurred to her that she might not like her daughter.

This thought was so awful and foreign that she could hardly even think it, let alone express it. She said she would like to know whether the analyst thought less of her now, but she would not ask this, because she had found out that such questions never got answered. To her surprise, the analyst said that it had been very helpful indeed to have had her express a personal feeling and particularly a hostile feeling. The patient said she felt flushed and red in the face. At this moment, she was experiencing some very personal feelings of her own, and the analyst emphasized this fact because she was usually not aware of the individuality of her emotions. Since the analyst expressed no feelings, her own stood out in stark relief. In her own words, she was alone and there was "somebody there."

The patient had come face to face with some of her own hostile feelings and had discovered, through the analyst's neutrality, that she was the one who had censored these emotions, not the analyst. Later in the same session, an opportunity presented itself to comment on her hesitation to begin each session—another illustration of unrecognized hostile or aggressive feelings. Since the patient had been able to express hostility against her daughter, it was then not so difficult for her to admit some negative feelings about the analysis.

At the end of the session, the patient said that she felt as if a great burden had been lifted from her chest, and she asked, musingly, how she ever had got to this point. She was as surprised at the end of her session as some readers might be at the end of this chapter to realize that all this material had come from a casual and "superficial" chance remark about another patient she had met in the waiting room. There had been no soul-searching and no digging, no "finding myself" nor talk about the unconscious or symbols. The patient had merely said everything that happened to cross the surface of her mind: she had associated freely.

FIVE

.

The Patient and His Family

While the process of inner reorganization takes place, the patient's life outside the analyst's office has to go on as usual. The patient is somewhat in the position of a storekeeper during inventory time, when files are emptied, stocks are being counted, and everything is out of place, yet customers keep coming and have to be taken care of. If he could, the patient might want to carry a sign reading, "During alterations, business as usual." And just as the necessary, temporary disorder during rebuilding or inventory creates some confusion and disrupts the normal working-day routine, so the patient, like the storekeeper, finds himself somewhat bewildered, irritated, and often less efficient in his work and disturbed in his relations with his family.

To make this quite clear, we might take the patient who had just discovered that perhaps she did not always like her daughter. If we could follow her from the analytic session sketched at the end of the previous chapter, into her home and her relationship with her daughter and husband, we might see quite clearly that "Business as usual" is not always possible.

Her daughter is now twelve years old. For all of her twelve

years she has done as she pleased. Her mother has never been able to set limits for her or refuse any request or help her bear any frustration. We know that the mother, who had felt there was nobody there when she was alone, needed the daughter so that she could feel alive and real. It was inevitable that the daughter grew up to be a "spoiled, indulged child," as her relatives and teachers put it. The father, who, at the beginning of his marriage had been enchanted by his wife's devotion and utter dependency on him, had grown weary of having, as he put it, two daughters at home. He had withdrawn from the family and invested all his devotion and energy in his work. As far as his daughter was concerned, he left her education up to his wife and good schools.

On the afternoon following her analytic session, the mother felt a little bewildered and yet alive with the first taste of a new freedom. As she opened the door to her apartment, she was struck by a blast of rock-and-roll music, accented by the rhythmic stamping of many feet. Her daughter was having a party. The front hall was littered with coats, books, boots. A trail of potato chips led from the living room into the kitchen, where ice cubes, empty Coke bottles, and soiled glasses covered the counters.

None of this was unusual. Her daughter often brought friends home from school, and their behavior today was no different from other afternoons. What was different was the mother's reaction to it. Without taking off her coat, she walked into the living room and stood by the door. The daughter and some of her friends gave her their customary casual "Hi" and went on chanting the tune at the top of their voices.

As she stood there quietly, she was assailed by a flood of conflicting feelings—scorn for the careless indifference of her daughter and her friends, guilt about her newly discovered feelings of anger, old fears of losing her lifeline, and new hope for her own independence. Her head began to hurt, and she called out with what she thought to be force and wrath, "Please turn down the record player." In reality, her voice was as soft and subdued as ever, much too quiet for the shrieks of the youngsters and the blare of the record. But one of the young people who had passed her at that moment caught something in her expression and stopped to ask, "Did you say something?"

Cornered, and unable to withdraw, the mother repeated her request, which was passed along and led to the desired action. Quite suddenly, the room was quiet. The daughter, who had been unaware of her mother's request, rushed to the record player to turn it up again, berating whoever had turned it down. But some of her friends objected. "Your mother has a headache—she wants us to turn it down low."

Now it was the daughter who stood still and faced her mother across the room in utter amazement and cold anger. "My mother said that?"

None of her friends could see anything startling in the request. They wanted to know what the big deal was all about— why couldn't they go on with the sound turned down? The daughter had to admit that apparently there was nothing unreasonable about the request, but somehow she could not go on with the party. Something was happening that she could not understand.

A short time later, the young people left and the daughter, on the way to her room, slipped and fell over some potato chips. Why was there such a mess, she said. Nobody had bothered to clean it up. This had never happened before. What was the matter with her mother anyway? Sitting in her room, with the door closed, she waited for her mother to come and ask about her.

She started her homework, waiting all the time for her mother to come, as she always did, with a glass of milk, but her mother did not appear. Then she remembered that her mother had behaved strangely at the party and had said something about having a headache. That was the answer—her mother was sick. She went out of her room and was amazed to find the mess of the party untouched and her mother sitting by the window in her bedroom reading.

"You aren't sick?" she asked belligerently. When her mother shook her head, the girl went into action. What was the idea spoiling her party, not giving her a hand with cleaning up? Why, she had nearly broken a leg and how come her mother just sat there? At first her mother remained firm, sensing the effect of the inner change, but after the daughter had kept up her attack long enough and had burst into tears and a violent temper tantrum, the mother gave up and reverted to her old habits. Torrents of guilt washed over her budding awareness of self, dragging her down. She sensed vaguely that she still had a long way to go in her analysis.

A short time later, however, a subtle change in her behavior was noted by her husband. Husband and daughter compared notes and decided that mother was getting worse. There was only one explanation—the analysis.

The patient was now experiencing the common opposition from husband or family that occurs frequently throughout the course of an analysis. Though she carried on her usual chores, the manner in which she did them was apparently different enough to have an effect on her family. The patient had suffered for a very long time before beginning analysis, but her family had made an adjustment to her neurotic behavior, without realizing that this was not the best way for her to live. The daughter, for example, could not possibly know why her mother had never been firm with her. She had always lived with a mother who assured her of her love and never said no. This had seemed as natural to the daughter as the color of her mother's eyes, or the home in which she lived. It had been her reality. Of course she resented the change and opposed it in every way she could. The husband was not very pleased with his wife's changed behavior either. She suddenly seemed to be developing a mind of her own.

All kinds of little things were happening. One day she refused to watch a television program they had enjoyed together for years. Another day she insisted on going to bed before the late-news program. She talked about taking a course at the university, and she dropped an old friend. What's going on around here, the husband demanded to know, and he expressed his complaints: "Until this started, we had no secrets from each other—at least she had no secrets from me. Now she goes to this analyst and talks everything over with him. Does she tell me what's bothering her? No, sir—she tells him. I know the guy is qualified and has all kinds of degrees and all that—but, still and all, he's a man and from what I can gather, he's not even bad-looking. How would you feel if your wife went to see a handsome man every day practically, and told him the most confidential things? I mean, everything—no holds barred. In fact, she is not to leave anything out in what she spills there and, frankly, I don't like it. I get to feel I'm never alone with my wife any more ever—there's always the shadow of the other man. It's being in bed with two people, and the other one is a man who is God in her eyes. His word is law in my house. I've nothing to say any more. All I'm allowed to do is to pay the guy. Isn't that ironical?"

The husband's jealousy, his anger and resentment, are perfectly reasonable. From where he stands, his wife's analysis is a very disturbing and aggravating thing. While these disturbances will most likely lead to a healthier state for the individuals and the family, the process will not always be painless or without upheavals.

This mother did not go into analysis because of her concern over her relationship with her daughter or husband; she went because of a general feeling of helplessness, depression, and anxiety.

That the effects of her analysis showed directly at home, in the prescribed way, was a secondary effect. It is more complicated if a patient goes into analysis because of concern over relationships with family or spouse.

A young and successful businesswoman had married a somewhat younger man, a gifted artist without an income but with a high earning potential. She got much satisfaction from mothering her attractive husband, taking care of him in every way, including financially—until he began to have affairs. During many evenings of bitter talk, she recognized that not only her husband but she herself needed help. Yet, having taken the main responsibility for the marriage, she insisted that he be the first to get himself straightened out, since he was the one who had disrupted their relationship. He fought bitterly against any kind of therapy, insisting that his behavior was his form of "freedom," necessary for his "artistic temperament." He accused his wife of dominating him, and refused to accept any responsibility for himself or his behavior. The relationship deteriorated until the wife announced that she was going to ask for a divorce unless he went into analysis. She enumerated his problems, including his sexual perversions, his inability to complete any work, his lack of responsibility in their home. She told him that she had not lost any of her original belief in him but was certain that without some profound character changes, he would never amount to anything, as either an artist or a person.

She offered to pay for his analysis, and the husband began treatment, feeling that he had nothing to lose. He had somewhat the same attitude that young people whose parents or counsellors insist that they undertake analysis have. While the analyst felt from the start that the man would get much more out of his analysis if he put some of his own efforts into it, and that therefore he ought to pay for some of it himself, it was clear that such a demand would have been premature for this man, who always had lived off other people—family, foundations, relatives, and now his wife. There would have been no realistic motivation for him to earn his own money or contribute some toward his analysis. Becoming financially responsible would have to be part of his becoming responsible in all ways. It could not have any meaning for him until he himself had recognized the necessity for it.

And, just as parents often feel they have the right to inquire into the lives of their children, since they are paying for their education or therapy, so the wife of this patient inquired into the progress of his analysis. In some ways, she took a very understandably active part in it, but unknowingly she was interfering with the very results for which she was hoping.

Not that she asked her husband direct questions. She was too sophisticated and alert to become an open target of his hostility. On the contrary, she assured him on many occasions that she was not going to "butt in," be nosy or inquisitive. Her interference was much less open or even conscious. What she did was to observe him for visible changes, the way one watches a sick child for the effect of medication: "Is he getting better?"

If there were some minor behavior changes, she commented on them by way of praise and approval. When, on one occasion, he went to the kitchen to do the dishes, she was enthusiastic. "How nice," she would say. "You have never done that before!"

This kind of condescending approval of his improvement naturally made him angry. More and more, he felt like a child living with a doting and controlling parent. "She pays for the analysis," he would say. "She thinks she is responsible for the results—she wants the rewards for her money." He got tired of taking her money for his analysis and for his whole support. By then he had experienced the need for further treatment and no longer wanted to give the analysis up. For the first time he felt the need to support himself in more ways than one. To his surprise, he encountered heavy opposition to his plan to get a job in the commercial-art field. The opposition came from his wife. She suggested that it would interfere with both his analysis and his creative work, that it would blunt his sensitivity and his style. She would be delighted to finance his expenses; in fact, nothing would give her more pleasure. This was unfortunately an understatement—as she discovered in her own analysis years later. Keeping him dependent and tied to her in this manner was one of the most important satisfactions of her life.

It was at this point in his analysis that his wife began to interfere openly. She urged him to give it up. In spite of the glaring contradiction—the fact that she had encouraged him to begin analysis—he continued, to the accompaniment of his wife's increasing attacks. "Your analyst is trying to fit you into a routine mold," she would say. "He is trying to make an average person out of you—a good Joe."

Some of these well-timed attacks hit their target and bothered her husband, since they were expressions of some of his remaining doubts about himself and what analysis would do to him. While he ridiculed her comments, he took some of them to heart and expressed them in his analysis. His wife's support of his irrational fears strengthened his rationalizations and increased his resistance. The interference was not crucial, since he was able to continue to associate and work through his insights, but his case, like the previous one, may help to clarify some of the complex aspects of interplay between the patient and his family.

If treatment progresses satisfactorily, there will be more objectivity on the part of the patient, a greater awareness of himself and the ways in which he has used and been used by others. The brief episode in the home of the patient who saw her daughter's behavior more objectively, for example, raises the next question: What does the mother's changing attitude do to her daughter and husband? Or, in the case of the business executive and her artist husband: What will the effect be on his wife as he takes more responsibility? In other words, while we have remained entirely patient-centered until now, and have, in this chapter, considered the effect of the family on the patient, we cannot overlook the converse aspect of this issue: *What is the effect of the patient's analysis on his family?*

The initial annoyance or jealousy, the impatience and yet gladness about changes have been briefly mentioned. But, in reality, the effects of an analysis on the family are more involved than that. For illustrations of this complexity, let us take the same family members whom we have seen as they affect the patient. What happens, for example, to the daughter of the patient, or to the wife of the artist?

The daughter is just now going through one of the most difficult phases of growth—adolescence. In addition, there is the particular complication of having to grow up with a fairly uninterested father, and a mother who was afraid to be firm. It is well known that the absence of wholesome firmness is as weakening to the personality as harshness, so that the daughter went into adolescence with some particular handicaps.

At the very moment of her life when children normally reach out for greater independence, her mother suddenly became assertive and made demands she had never made before. All at once, the daughter was asked to clean up her own mess, to pay attention to her mother's headache. While she had never had to account for her goings and comings, at this point, when her friends were sharing less and less with their mothers, this girl's mother was asking for more contact and response. Nothing could have been more confusing for the daughter—and yet, as we know from the mother's analysis, the development was unavoidable. If this daughter complained that her mother did not understand her, she had greater reason than most young people. It is not too difficult to imagine that she might accuse her mother of inconsistency and unfairness.

This will, of course, have its effect on her mother and on the progress of her analysis. The mother may become quite disturbed over her newly found freedom and retreat from the reasonable attacks of her daughter—not to mention the barrages from her husband. She may consider giving up analysis, reasoning that it does more harm than good, upsetting her whole family and making everybody miserable. As she expresses these doubts at home, husband and daughter will feel guilty at having interfered in mother's treatment and retreat in turn.

There is a visible chain reaction resulting from the personality changes that occur in analysis. Sometimes one of the results of this interaction is the discovery of the hidden problems of family members. Triggered by the mother's behavior, the daughter in this situation had to recognize that all was not well in her own life—not only in her relationship with mother but in other relationships as well. When these disturbing discoveries seemingly coincided with several talks with her home-room teacher at school, it became clear that the daughter had not been functioning well for a long time.

There had been straws in the wind for more than two years, but since the mother handled them with self-blame, the daughter had continued to withdraw from meaningful relationships. Now that the mother was more aware of her own role in the family, she could consider discussing her daughter's problems less defensively with the guidance counsellor at school. The idea of using the child guidance services available in the community was no longer a preposterous one but could be considered with some objectivity. After an exploratory study by the school psychologists, including the standard tests and initial interviews, the school and family agreed that the daughter could benefit from some psychological help.

In this case, while the mother's analysis had had some disturbing influences on the family, it also led to some necessary help for the daughter. In the other case, the effects of the husband's analysis on the wife were more upsetting. The wife's problems came into the open when her artist husband, who was the patient, accused her of getting her satisfactions from dominating him. Nothing could have been more upsetting to her, for in her capacity as a business executive she had always been afraid of playing just this role as a woman.

As the oldest child of a large family that her father had deserted when she was quite young, she had had to take responsibility for her younger brothers and sisters long before she was ready for it. She had to learn to become efficient, run the house, take care of the smaller children, until this became, instead of a chore, one of her successful accomplishments. When she was still in high school, her mother was stricken with a prolonged and fatal illness, so that she felt she had to be mother and father to her siblings. It was understood that she had to take care of herself as well, and she became self-sufficient as a matter of urgent necessity. This, together with a very early and strong attachment to her father, was to become part of her character.

This is not the place to give a picture of the inner development of this woman, but even the outer factors suffice to help understand her strong doubts about her femininity and her deep and repressed competition with men. In spite of her careful grooming, chic wardrobe, and feminine beauty, her doubts about her role as a woman and a wife were continuously with her. When, for example, she learned of her husband's affairs, she immediately took this as another sign of her lack of femininity and attractiveness. While she never would admit it to herself openly, she suffered from the anxious fear that without her financial power, her husband would not remain with her. These fears were carefully covered up with a brisk, cheerful, and smiling manner, but they erupted violently when her husband—as a result of his analysis—told her what she had been afraid to face most of her adult life. Her denial and anger were vehement, but this time these feelings did not abate, as they had in the past.

Prior to his analysis, her husband had appeased her with charm or seduction, smoothing over the conflicts that existed between them. This had made it possible for her to forget about her latent insecurities and doubts. Now, however, her husband no longer found it necessary to avoid all conflicts. For many reasons, he needed to sharpen, rather than weaken, the differences between himself and his wife. While this occurred for only a brief period in his analysis, it was sufficiently disturbing for his wife to consider analytic help for herself. This idea came after she had experienced sleep disturbances for the first time in her life, and following a short detour into more than normal drinking. Her doubts continued to increase, affected her efficiency in her work, and shook the very foundation of her self-image. After many talks with friends, a brief affair, and increasing headaches, she finally saw no alternative but analysis.

Her first step, understandably, was to call her husband's analyst. (This is part of the topic of the patient and his family; indeed, in the treatment of children or young people, it may be one of the complicating factors, as we shall see shortly.) She found the first contact with the analyst disappointing and somewhat annoying. This is a reaction family members of patients frequently experience. It is a little like meeting somebody one has heard a great deal about. The wife of the artist had formed an image of her husband's analyst in her mind. His name had frequently been used in the past two years; she had learned to spell it correctly on the monthly checks and had laughed with her husband about the analyst. The patient had referred to his analyst on many occasions, quoting from the sessions, reporting whatever he could, sharing with his wife his indignation as well as his satisfactions about the analyst's interpretations. There had been many debates between husband and wife in which the analyst had figured prominently, as though he had been present as a third party. The woman felt she knew the analyst.

When she called, her fantasy about the analyst collided sharply with the reality. The man was friendly and distant, polite and noncommittal. Her feeling was, "He talks as though we were strangers"; then came the correction, "But we really are strangers." This was not somebody with whom she could discuss her feelings about herself and her husband, this was not a friend of the family —this quite clearly was her husband's analyst. In the manner of his speech and in the content, the friendly distance was maintained; while she used her husband's first name, the analyst referred to him as "your husband." She mentioned a few recent episodes with which the analyst—she assumed—was familiar, but from his response she could not tell whether he knew what she was talking about. While she was perfectly willing to discuss even intimate details with him, his response was so noncommittal that she could not even be sure he knew her husband. It seemed strange to her that this man was intent on revealing nothing, on keeping his contact with the patient strictly confidential, while she was ready to talk to him like the old friend she felt he was. Besides, she was annoyed because she could not see why he acted as though she knew nothing about his patient. After all, she felt, I am his wife and not a nosy intruder. We do have something in common, this analyst and I. Why does he insist on acting as though I were an outsider?

It is difficult for members of the patient's family to appreciate, but from the analyst's point of view the wife *is* an outsider; indeed, the patient's whole family, past and present, is merely background, while the patient alone is the center of the analytic interest. It takes the patient some time to focus on himself as the center. Like his family, he tries to divert attention from his inner conflicts by talking not about his feelings for his wife but about his wife (or husband), her problems, hopes, and dreams. The analyst brings the patient back to the focus, himself—how he sees his wife, rather than how his wife sees him; his feelings about his children; his thoughts about anything in the world, as long as it is focused on himself. The patient would often prefer to analyze his wife or mother rather than himself; he finds it much easier to talk about the conflicts and shortcomings of important people in his life than to report on his own. The analyst makes it clear to him that in this office and this analytic relationship, the patient alone is the issue, while his wife and how she started the argument is one of *her* problems. The wife is really an outsider, as far as the inner world of the unconscious mind is concerned, and at best in the supporting cast, as far as the conscious mind goes.

Besides this focus, the analyst knows that what he learns about the wife in passing is not objective but, rather, seen through the patient's mind. He is therefore aware of the fact that he doesn't know the wife at all, and he does not pretend to understand anything about her. Finally, there is the written and unwritten law about absolute confidentiality. The written aspect consists of the so-called "privileged communication," which gives the analyst the right, by law, to refuse to share any or all parts of his contact with the patient with a court of law. While this situation does not come up very often in practice, the unwritten law of confidentiality is tested continuously, and it is very important that patients can be perfectly sure nothing they talk about in their analysis will ever be revealed to anybody else.

These, then, are the reasons why the analyst talked as he did to the wife of the patient-artist. Nevertheless, the wife's visit to him remained disappointing to her for the reasons mentioned. She had called, after all, to talk about herself, and had mentioned her husband and their marital problems only to make the first contact. Once she got around to explaining that she, too, wanted to come for analysis, she reached the second hurdle, another characteristic difficulty with the family members of patients: the question of contact between the analyst and family members, whether brief or prolonged, leads finally to the question of whether one analyst can treat more than one member of the same family at one time.

Most analysts would agree that such a procedure could not be of maximum benefit to either patient. To have to share the analyst with one's marital partner complicates the analysis considerably, and sometimes brings it to a stop. The nature of confidentiality seems less of a safeguard if the husband-patient has to wonder whether his analyst may inadvertently reveal some of his hidden feelings to his wife when he sees her that afternoon for her analytic session. Since both partners will use the analyst for their own separate needs and will undoubtedly discuss their experiences with each other, their speculations about the analyst, what he has said or has not said; their possible use of him as a mediator in a conflict, all these act as interferences in a classical analysis.

There are, however, other forms of therapy, in which several members of a family are seen separately by the same doctor, or together. These will be discussed in a separate chapter.

In the case of the artist's wife, there was no real reason for her to choose her husband's analyst for herself. The issue here was not a marital conflict—a complication in the interaction between two people—but the resolution of deep and long-standing conflicts in her own psyche.

When her husband's analyst, at his patient's request, suggested the names of some colleagues for his wife, she began her analysis with one of them. For a short time, she wondered whether the two analysts got together to discuss her "case" or that of her husband. It was bad enough to share intimate and not always rational thoughts or feelings with one stranger, it was very unpleasant to think that this analyst was sharing any of her confidential material with her husband's analyst. When she brought up these fears in free association, what really had bothered her about the idea of two therapists sharing material became a little clearer. She recognized that she would have had no objection whatsoever if her family physician had talked with her gynecologist about an operation she had had some time back. But two analysts talking about her did bother her, partly because one was her husband's analyst. It appeared that she had certain feelings about the other analyst, who, she believed, had formed an unfair picture of her. She had originally wanted to go to him for analysis so that she could tell "her side of the story," and she felt that now he would retain this unfair picture and even influence her own analyst. She had thought of her husband's analyst as a judge, an authority, perhaps a parental figure before whom she was unjustly accused. When she could not get her "day in court"—when the first analyst did not take her on—she remained angry and hostile, and felt that her analyst should have nothing more to do with the other, "unco-operative" therapist.

The whole constellation reminded her of a time in her childhood when her younger brother—one year her junior—had complained about her management of the family to their mother. The patient had the same feeling now as she had then: "He got there first, and I don't have the chance to tell my side of the story."

While such a carry-over of feelings from the past would have been analyzed in any case, it was much easier for her to do this with a stranger who knew neither her husband nor herself. It is not difficult to imagine how she would have used her husband's analyst for a period of time: She would have felt it necessary to explain her behavior, to correct the impression that she felt her husband had given of her, to ask for assurance and present endless countercharges. She would have been apt to use any reassuring comment by the analyst as a justification of herself, and to employ it herself in the evening as a weapon against her husband: "You see, even your analyst says . . ." The husband, in turn, would have felt it necessary to defend himself, to bring this material back to his analyst—all unnecessary detours in his own analysis.

The process of re-experiencing, which we emphasized in previous chapters, is clearly not aided if the analyst works concurrently with members of one's own family or close relatives. It is natural for a patient who has a good analytic experience to want to have the same analyst see the people close to him, but the disadvantages far outweigh the positive aspects. As one patient who had had such an experience in the past put it, "The business gets messy."

Another very common complication between patient and family arises when a marriage partner sees his mate changing in a direction with which he cannot see himself going along. We may suppose, for example, that the wife of the artist had not been willing to consider her own difficulties, had not found it necessary to do something herself, but had instead become increasingly resentful about her husband's changes. This situation is not uncommon and is in part responsible for the resentful attitude many people have toward analysis.

If a marriage such as this one had been is based on a precarious, neurotic balance, major changes in the personality structure of one partner will upset the balance. With the basis for the relationship eliminated or considerably changed, the whole relationship may disintegrate. Had the young business executive not been able to consider her own problems, it is entirely possible that the marriage would not have continued. The artist husband might have found himself in a position where he could no longer accept his wife in the same way as he had before his analysis. Nothing would be more understandable, but his wife's bitter resentment against him and his analysis would result in cynical and bitter declarations that all the analysis had done was to wreck her marriage.

She would present a reasonable-sounding case. She would be able to say that their marriage was not ideal but that they had been happy until her husband started playing around. To stop this, she had spent a great deal of money and put up with many difficult years—only to be left without a husband. If she was a person who could not see her own problems, she would also resent the personality changes in her husband. She would still want to see him as he was before his analysis, and she would describe his changes in a negative way. Yes, she would say, he has changed, but not for the better. He was a charming, somewhat easygoing boy who was carefree and full of fun. It was a pleasure to wait on him and take care of his every need, but now he resents it if I mix into his business. Instead of spending his time going to museums and attending sketching classes, he has taken a job in the commercial-art field and insists on making as much money as possible. He is painting on his own, but he wants his own one-man show, is no longer content with an obscure group show, craves recognition, has given up his quaint way of dressing, and looks like any businessman—in short, he is a changed person. If this is what analysis does, she would say, he can have it.

In other words, the family of the patient may not always accept the changes that come about through the therapeutic process; instead, analysis becomes the object of blame.

The same problem of using analysis as a scapegoat comes up frequently when the family finds itself affected by the analysis of one of its members, without being directly involved. A fairly typical illustration of this can be found whenever a patient announces his inability while in analysis to make a major change in his life, such as a shift of jobs, getting married or divorced. While no other member of the family is in any way connected with the therapy, a young girl's declaration that she cannot get married next June may cause considerable distress to her fiancé and her own family. The most natural whipping boy will be the analyst.

While there is no absolute law, it is usually considered wise not to make either major changes or long-term commitments while in analysis, because it is reasonable to assume that patients will frequently have different requirements for close contacts or for major activities after changes of the personality than they had before or during the process. This cannot be a general rule because for some patients this does not hold. But usually patients find themselves in a strange position during the analytic process—they have the impression that some of their close friends are changing. As their own unconscious needs are analyzed, they are no longer acted out with current figures, so that in reality it is they who are behaving differently—a process no more noticed by them than physical growth is noticed in adolescence. The typical adolescent's reaction is, "Mother, you have suddenly become smaller," and something like this occurs with the psychological changes in analysis. If, for example, a patient had a strong need to help out everybody he knew, he would have been drawn to people who appreciated his intense helpfulness; indeed, this may have been one of the attractions in the relationship. During his analysis, the patient may discover that this tendency to help out at every opportunity is one way to obligate people and to cover up the fear of antagonizing them. As such a trait is gradually analyzed, as its constituent parts are uncovered, the patient will gradually be more selective in his helping-out behavior. He may feel free to refuse certain favors to old friends, and these old friends, in turn, will withdraw a little from him. The patient will say, "I wonder why Jim has not called all week; he used to be on my neck all the time and pour out his heart. What happened to Jim? That he had expressed his self-interest to Jim in very subtle ways in the last few contacts will have escaped him; he will notice only the changed reaction in Jim.

If one considers that not only one character trait but some very basic behavior patterns may change during analysis, it is understandable that the analyst usually advises patients not to make long-range commitments during the process. It would not be too difficult for the patient to accept Jim's slight withdrawal; in fact, he may welcome it. But it would pose a major problem if it were his fiancée who could not accept the changes in him, or if the patient could not accept behavior in her which he never questioned before analysis. As an illustration, let us take the family of a young woman who had been regularly seeing a young man in analysis. In this case, the young man had come from abroad and been without his own family, except for an aunt and a few cousins with whom he was not too close. Quite naturally, he had adopted the girl's family as his own and was considered by them as a member of the family. There had been no question that the two young people would eventually get married. The family knew the young man was in treatment. They considered this necessary because of the tragic way in which he had lost his parents in Europe, and they saw nothing disturbing about his having some problems. In fact, they were proud of him for having the courage to work them out with professional help.

The family was intelligent, liberal, co-operative, and quite willing to wait with the final wedding arrangements until the young man's finances were in satisfactory shape. After all, they said, he had come here without a penny, had to catch up on his studies, needed to establish himself in his field; it was understandable that he didn't want to make definite commitments until he could afford a wife and a home. While the family was well able to help the young couple financially, they respected his wish to take care of his own home once he was ready, and did not press him or their daughter.

For about two years, the young people went out together, and the family saw nothing wrong in their intimacies because it was only a matter of time before they would be married. By the time the young man was thirty—in fact, during his birthday party—the first clouds appeared. A relative of the family, a jovial and good-natured family physician, made some joking references during the party to the age at which people should have children. While it was not clear whether he had meant to refer to the young couple, it was taken up by the daughter as a "dig" against her fiancé. Without having been challenged, she came to his defense. She declared that they would get married and have children when she and her fiancé were ready for it, and not before. The intensity with which she spoke revealed to everyone her troubled feelings about the future. Later that night, the young man asked her about it, and, to his surprise, he found her near tears when he brought up the whole subject of marriage and the future. It appeared that behind her reasonable and permissive exterior there had been a smoldering resentment against the uncertainty and against his analysis. It came out quite against her will and was as much a surprise to her as to him.

In a way, the young woman felt, the family physician had been quite right—she should not wait much longer to get married and raise a family, since she was going on thirty herself. She asked, perhaps for the first time with that much insistence, that they set a wedding date, even if it were a distant one. She felt that the uncertainty was not good for her, and she added, with bitterness, that even his analyst ought to be able to understand this.

The young man now did what patients in analysis often do —he used the analyst to hide his own conflicts. He tried to blame him for standing in the way of his marriage plans and seemed to concur in his fiancée's indignation about this interference. He made out the usual analytic suggestion—to postpone permanent commitments—to be an inflexible law. When the patient associated to this experience in his analytic hour, the analyst asked him whether he felt that he was ready for marriage now. The patient admitted that he felt very guilty about the girl's wonderful family, but, in truth, he was not sure that he wanted to marry at all for the time being. His real wish was to finish his studies, to live in different parts of the country, to have many and different experiences, rather than to settle down. In time, he became free enough to be honest with the girl and her family, but it is doubtful whether they could ever get over the suspicion that all this was, in reality, the analyst's fault.

Again, as with the wife of the artist, the process of therapy had not caused the change in the relationship between the young people, but it could be used as an object of blame.

The same problem comes up in more pronounced ways in the therapy of adolescents who are still living with their families. Parents sometimes expect certain changes to occur in the process of therapy, and tend to hold the analyst responsible if the changes do not take the desired form. Young people may use their therapist to avoid certain responsibilities at home, like the fiancé of the young woman. Frequently, parents of adolescent or younger patients find direct contact with the therapist necessary and, because of the patient's age and dependency relationship, therapists sometimes see some member of the family. This, in turn, has repercussions on the therapeutic process, which is one of the many special problems in the general category of young patients and their families. Another special problem is the modification of analytic techniques that is often necessary in work with children and young people. The following chapter is about these and other special aspects of therapy with children and adolescents.

SIX

·

Analytic Therapy with Children and Youth

The title of this chapter suggests that when it comes to children and young people, analytic techniques are usually modified because a full analysis requires, as was pointed out in the first chapter, a relatively well-developed ego. In childhood and adolescence, it is not always possible to differentiate the continuous inner changes in body and mind from the neurotic conflicts. For example, one does not always know whether prolonged moodiness is a normal adolescent disturbance, requiring not so much therapy as time to grow up, or whether it is the result of deeper, unresolved inner conflicts. For this reason, the analytic goals are often more limited and the techniques modified, yet the emphasis is still on psychoanalysis. There are, of course, a great many nonanalytic ways in which children and young people can be helped—remedial reading, counselling, child guidance, and group therapy. We will take up other forms of therapy in a later chapter; here we will continue to discuss analysis, though in modified form, for children and young people.

The modification of analytic techniques is not the only thing that is different when it comes to young people. The relationship between the analyst and the patient's family is different. So are the patient's financial responsibility, the frequency of sessions, and the manner of communication between analyst and patient.

All of these points can be observed in the beginning phase of treatment of a bright fifteen-year-old boy who was referred to the analyst by his private school because of his extremely destructive behavior. He would upset cans of paint in the art shop, seemingly by accident; he would tip over the projection camera from the balcony in the auditorium; he would write wrong answers in examinations and make sure that his hated neighbor would copy the wrong answers—that he himself failed in such tests was of secondary importance. In athletics, he would trip the running football player and laugh at the gasps of his teammates.

His marks were poor, except in subjects where he could succeed without working; his relationships with schoolmates were characterized by hostility and fear, except for a few fearful boys who admired him for his daring. The school had urged the family for some time to seek help for their only son, but the mother did not consider these actions more than childish pranks, and felt that they were for the school to handle.

After the school declared its inability to cope, the father agreed to step in. He was a physician, a general practitioner interested in psychotherapy and willing to try new, experimental ways. He had a few serious talks with his boy and, being a sophisticated community leader, decided to handle the situation a little differently. Harshness being out of the question for him and his indulgent wife, and reasoning having failed to curb the boy, the father embarked on a project of his own. He admitted to his son that he did not understand adolescents, and proposed that they discuss the son's problems and the father's problems together, tape-record their sessions, and then attempt to publish a new kind of book on father-son relations in the turbulent years of adolescence.

The boy had no objection, and the next few months were devoted to the new project. The father gave up his own hobbies, and every evening after supper father and son sat down for their talks. Father asked searching questions, and the son gave candid answers. Since the destructive acts in school had precipitated this project, much of their discussion centered around the boy's hostility. To the father's surprise, the son did not hesitate to describe in gory detail his sadistic fantasies, his pleasure in being destructive, his cunning schemes to deceive the authorities and get ahead in the world by outsmarting the next fellow and hitting before he could be hurt himself. The reels of tape piled up, and the father —whose early ambition had been to write—enjoyed the prospect of an interesting manuscript.

In the meantime, the boy's behavior in school continued unabated. His destructive acts became more serious, his marks fell further down, and the director of the school, unaware of the father's secret project, insisted on professional help as a condition of the student's remaining in the school.

The father was the first to make contact with the analyst. He presented a very intelligent picture of his son, laced with professional lingo and as detached as if he were talking about a patient, rather than his own child. Next came the mother, who was clearly upset by this development. She spoke of her husband's writing project, which she considered foolish, blamed herself for having been too easy with her boy, and offered her help in every possible way.

The patient, a stocky, bright-looking lad, was ready for anything, and began his first session by taking out of his pocket a small box that contained an assortment of sharp-pointed sewing needles. He explained to the analyst that he had these ready as potential weapons in fights with certain boys who might start something. He went on to explain his hostile acts in great detail, seemed to associate easily, and had no inhibition in admitting any of his activities.

Clearly, his purpose was to shock the therapist and to avoid co-operating by using a pseudo-co-operative manner of talking. After several such sessions, the analyst studied the notes he had made off and on during the weeks, and saw a pattern emerging: it seemed fairly clear that the boy was very deeply troubled by his great fears of being overwhelmed, by certain homosexual fantasies, and by an overwhelming hatred of all adults. He was actually unable to concentrate for any serious study, had no friends, no relationships with boys or girls, and needed therapy very much. There had been sleep disturbances of long standing and some physical symptoms that seemed to go beyond the usual adolescent skin disorders.

The boy was too frightened to co-operate, and needed his defensive armor. He could not associate but, instead, kept on talking in a marathon fashion, becoming suspicious when his therapist did not interrupt him. One day, he described a sadistic act in the gym, where he had managed to outwit the tallest basketball player. As he went on blithely recounting his adventure, the therapist interrupted him and said, "That this fellow is so tall really bothers you, doesn't it?"

The patient was below average size, and there was enough additional material to make the assumption that the height of his body and the status associated with it in adolescent society had some real meaning for him. He blushed slightly, stopped his recital and stared at the therapist, who told him that this had been the first comment of the patient's in which he had felt something.

"You mean," the boy said, "you knew all along that I was just talking?" The analyst nodded, and explained that he had been waiting for some expression of real feeling. He added that he had surmised the patient had not been ready to express anything of significance until now.

The boy put his elbows on the desk, dropped his round, friendly face into his cupped hands, and said, with a relieved grin, "I'll be damned!" After this, he really began to work. He described his father's evening project and explained that he had strung his father along.

"Boy, I gave him plenty of baloney."

"And," the therapist observed, "you did the same thing here."

"Yeah," the patient agreed, "except that it didn't work." He was delighted, like a small boy who has been running away from a parent until he is breathless and has been caught.

In quite a different tone, he told the therapist that he had to be awfully careful with people because one could never tell whom one could trust. The safest thing was to trust nobody. He felt that the way things were at home justified this thinking. Should he have trusted his father, when it was perfectly obvious to him that this writing nonsense was a form of blackmail? He had always known that his father was not particularly interested in him, or in children in general. Whenever his father did things with him, the boy said, he knew that it was a chore for his father. There had never been frankness. With his mother, it was the opposite— by being clever, he could get whatever he wanted from her.

"My mother thinks that everything is her fault. If you call her unfair, you can have the moon." Gradually, he brought out material that was less guarded, less prepared. One day, when he looked particularly tired, his therapist recalled the earlier reports about his sleep disturbances and waited for an opening to find some understanding of this symptom. The opportunity came when the boy yawned and remarked that he was beat today. The therapist asked, "Late to bed last night?" and the boy explained that no matter what time he went to bed, he had trouble falling asleep. By now, the relationship had been sufficiently established to permit the therapist to ask some open questions.

"What do you do when you can't fall asleep?" The boy told him that he often liked to do something to tire himself out. Among his favorite occupations was taking a tennis ball and banging it against the wall, catching it as though he were practicing his forehand in tennis. Any physical activity, he explained, tired him after a while.

As the therapist went into detail about this activity, it turned out that tennis was one of the competitive games he played with his father, with the fierce determination to beat him. It also became clear that the wall against which he banged his ball adjoined his parents' bedroom.

Eventually, after he had banged the ball long enough, one of his parents would wake up and come into his room. It was usually his mother. Because of her own anxiety and guilt over being an inadequate mother, she felt solicitous and stayed in his room for some time. The boy had succeeded in invading his parents' sleep or closeness, and getting his mother to leave her husband and, instead, come to him, sitting by his bedside and stroking his hands tenderly.

The deeper, sexual meanings of this behavior were not conscious for the patient. However, he did know that he meant to disturb his parents' sleep. It appeared that his hostile behavior was rewarded by his mother—who was equally unaware of the pattern into which she was falling.

In describing it at first, he used the phrase "I have to bang the ball," just as he had said that he "had to trip his friends in school" or "had to tip the projector over the balcony." The manner in which he described the episodes connected them; the sleep disturbances and the aggressive behavior were related: Both were hostile acts he "had" to perform. That he unconsciously meant to defeat a rival—father, teacher, another student, the school principal—was not at all clear to him at this phase of therapy. The key phrase, which gave the clue for the dynamics of his defense, was, "I had to." To him, it meant that he had no choice over this overt behavior, that it was, so to speak, happening inside of him and he was not responsible for it. By looking at this behavior as something he "had to do," he separated himself from his actions and kept himself free of gnawing guilt. He did not mean to do these things; he just "had to."

Since the patient was in danger of more serious delinquency, the urgent therapeutic task was to protect him from further acting out of his unconscious wishes. The therapist used some of the material on being dishonest in the family for this purpose. He referred back to this behavior—accepting for the moment the patient's view that the family had promoted dishonesty—and suggested that perhaps this had led the boy to be dishonest with himself.

"When you say you have to do these things, you are really kidding yourself, aren't you? It's a gimmick, like your father's book project." The patient gave a little when, after some initial anger against the wise-guy therapist, he admitted that he did not absolutely have to do all these things—they were just a lot of fun. The therapist said that he could see that it was fun for the patient, yet perhaps the patient did not absolutely have to have this kind of fun, but had some choice about it.

From this initial incision into his disturbed way of thinking to a modification of his outward behavior, several months' work was needed. Although the relationship with his therapist enabled the young patient to channel his aggressive behavior into more acceptable forms, such as competitive games, the school term drew to a close just as he discovered that he was gaining some control over his impulses, and his marks were not much better than they had been when he first came into therapy. While there was an improvement, there was some doubt about his promotion.

The patient brought this up in one of his sessions and asked the therapist to intervene for him with his teachers, since he was sure that the school, which had sent him into treatment, would pay attention to the therapist's recommendation about promotion. Because the therapist's entire success was based on a very candid, honest relationship, he took particular pains to emphasize this in this latest episode. He agreed with the boy that the school would probably consult him about promotion, but what did he, the patient, think about all this?

The boy's first reaction was characteristically impulsive—if he was not promoted, the school would ask him to leave. The therapist, who had by now developed a style of working with this young man, suggested that they consider this possibility together, as a theoretical idea. He asked whether the patient thought the school "had to" keep him. The patient, who by now had developed some ability to bear frustration and tension, did not blow up at such a challenging question. His second response was less impulsive. He considered this a funny question on the therapist's part, but on the other hand it was not exactly a crazy question, either. It was quite true that the school did not absolutely have to keep him. He now looked back at his school record and summed it up by saying, "I have not done much more than fool around. This school makes it easy to do that."

He was, in a way, expressing some insight that was not yet fully conscious. He was saying that, at school as at home, he needed more firmness. He was being objective when he observed that the atmosphere of the school was entirely too free for him, duplicating in some way his mother's behavior. That this was really threatening to him, he had before now only felt; now he could consider it more objectively.

The therapist suggested that perhaps this was not the best school for him. The patient concurred, asking, "You mean they are not strict enough?"

He was, in fact, asking for more firmness from authority figures than he had been getting all his life. At the same time, he was beginning to face some of the results of his destructive and self-destructive behavior in school and at home. In his recognition that he needed more limits than he had had in the past, he was also recognizing some of his inner problems—the strength of his impulses and his inability to cope with them.

The therapist and the patient, after a few sessions, agreed that this school was not the best place for him and, after some conferences with parents and teachers, a transfer to a less permissive school was made. Since the boy entered this new school with the attitude of having to succeed by hard work, his original symptoms no longer appeared, so that it was now possible for the therapist to begin to work on the deeper layers of his problems. In a way, the work up to this point had been preparatory to more intensive analytic work.

This is one of the fairly typical differences between adult analysis and young people's analytic therapy. While some adults may also require a preparatory educational phase prior to actual analytic work, it is almost always necessary with adolescents. Another difference is the informal, give-and-take atmosphere illustrated in this case. The patient does not use the couch, and the analyst is not unobtrusive but quite active. The communication is not via free association in the strict analytical sense, but consists of direct, face-to-face discussions. The relationship between the analyst and the patient's family is clearly much more direct than in the adult cases discussed in the previous chapter.

The analytic goals, however, are the same. The unconscious wishes and instinctual demands in the boy's case were just becoming visible. They had been covered by a disturbing symptom— insomnia. While this young patient was quite aware of his sadistic acts in school and at home, he was quite unaware of the deeper meaning of these acts. The difference between deliberate deception and unconscious resistance was visible. When he reported his sadistic acts toward his father, or acted them out with the therapist in the first few sessions, he was consciously pretending, playing a delaying game; but his banging the ball against his parents' bedroom was not a stalling maneuver at all. In the latter case, he did not know what he was doing. If a naïve therapist had told him that this was an unconscious sexual and aggressive wish acted out in the form of a ball game, the boy would have laughed it off and denied the interpretation, because he was not conscious of the hidden motivations. He may become conscious of them if he begins a full analysis in which all the steps leading to the onset of these demands can be traced back and re-experienced via the relationship with the analyst, who will then take on the more unobtrusive, listening role necessary for this analytic experience.

Is it possible for the young patient to adjust to the new role his therapist will have to play once he is ready for a full analysis? Often this shift is possible, since it has been gradual, but in some cases young patients have been referred to a different analyst after they have had this preparatory experience. Usually, there is a time interval between the preparatory phase and the full analysis, sometimes of several years' duration. This time span is often necessary because of the rapidly changing personality structure of adolescents. It also makes it possible for the analyst to evaluate the necessity for a full analysis.

In the case of this boy, for example, analysis would have been desirable because, when he was seen three years later, his earlier patterns of behavior had not been basically modified. While he had graduated from the second school, and had done well in his work and his relationship to his schoolmates, he was now expressing his unconscious hostility in his contacts with girls. He was choosing girls who wanted to be dominated or even hurt, and was developing some sexual perversions in which his sadistic needs were clearly expressed. Without inflicting pain on a girl, he could have no sexual satisfactions. His relationships were violent and of short duration, and there had been one very unpleasant episode in which a particularly nice girl had become pregnant because of his carelessness and hostility.

In spite of all this, the young man, for a number of reasons, did not see the need for analysis at this time. But he came back to it several years later, after his second marriage broke up.

The natural question arises: Could this unhappy development have been avoided by keeping him in therapy while he was still an adolescent? This tricky question has been debated by practitioners of analysis and by human-relations experts in general for a long time. Clearly, there is no easy answer. Sometimes it is not possible to keep children or adolescents in therapy; sometimes it has been done. In the case of this boy, it might have been possible, were it not for the family involvements that always play a major part in the therapy of children and young people. The analyst had recommended continuation of treatment and the parents had not openly opposed it. When the question of transfer to another school had arisen, the mother had campaigned for a particularly well-known junior college, which happened to be located too far out of town to make continuation of therapy possible. Without doubt, the school had a great many advantages over the available schools in town, but the choice of this better school also meant discontinuation of analysis. When the analyst was asked whether analysis was absolutely necessary—in fact, so urgent that a good school had to be sacrificed—he had to say no. There was no question that a full analysis was indicated, but it seemed reasonable at the time to suggest that it could wait until the patient had had the advantage of an excellent school. There had been no overt symptoms at the time, there had been no visible indications of the immediate need for analysis, and it would have been hard for the patient and his family to believe that there was absolute, clear-cut urgency.

This is one answer to the question, could this unhappy development have been avoided? The answer apparently is yes and no. And this, in itself, points to another characteristic of the analytic therapy of children and adolescents—the difficulty of accurate predictions. This difficulty is in part due to the special factors present in their lives. One could isolate a number of such special factors: A young person is leaving his old family and preparing himself for his own future family; he is still financially and emotionally dependent on his parents and resentful of this dependency; his involvement with his parents triggered off the symptoms of which he is aware as he enters therapy or analysis; his need for privacy is pronounced and his relationship to the future therapist is in part contingent upon the degree of confidentiality the patient can hope for; his feelings of guilt about his hostility, and his ambivalence about the need for privacy, will complicate his readiness to enter a new relationship separate from the family.

The family is equally in a state of conflict, also determined by the role of parents of adolescents: The parents' intellectual readiness to trust their adolescent to another adult conflicts with their feelings of rivalry with the therapist; their wish to have the adolescent work out his problems is tinged with the fear that these problems are in part caused by themselves; their readiness for financial responsibility is mixed with doubt over the necessity for this expense, whose outcome is so uncertain; their desire for a healthy adolescent is overshadowed by their own concept of health and values, which may be different from that of the therapist.

The involvement with the family and the ways in which young patients use parents while in therapy is illustrated by the case, discussed in the previous chapter, of the twelve-year-old girl whose mother was in analysis. We showed some of the effects of the mother's analysis on the daughter when the mother came home from one of her sessions and found young people having a party in the living room. We mentioned that, as a result of the mother's analysis, the daughter had seen the guidance counsellor in school.

Because of the difficulty in predicting developments in adolescence, the counsellor consulted an analyst to discuss the possibility of more intensive analytic work with the girl. While both workers agreed that therapy was indicated, the question of predicting her behavior remained; in particular, the question of how much of her behavior was a normal adolescent disturbance and how much was to be considered pathology.

To show this typical difficulty in analytic work with adolescents, some of the therapist's thinking will be included in the following description, and the girl's case will be used for two purposes—to illustrate both the complex family interaction in therapy with adolescents, and one of the technique problems typical for patients at this phase of development.

Among other problems, the girl had a persistent habit of coming home late from dates or parties. This is, of course, a characteristic teen-age problem, and taken by itself it would be of no particular interest in our discussion. But it can be used as a starting point into the two areas to be illustrated—special family involvements and analytic techniques with adolescents.

After weeks of calm debate and angry argument, the daughter had agreed with her parents to be home no later than midnight after a Saturday-evening party. On the particular Saturday in question, the occasion was the birthday party of the boy whom she considered her special date. Many members of her crowd were present. Each of the youngsters had a deadline, but none admitted to it, so that they could tell their parents later that the others didn't have to go home. There was some rivalry between the daughter and another girl for the host, and the daughter was very certain that to go home at the appointed time would mean the end of her romance. It was extremely important to her to outstay the other girl, and as the clock kept going around, she managed to forget about her agreement with her parents. When the boy's parents called time and reminded her of her own parents, she felt guilty but found solace in the thought of her therapist, who, she was sure, would "understand." No matter what her father—who she knew could get very angry—might do, there was always her therapist, who would take her side. She finally got into the car of another boy at close to two o'clock in the morning, and started on her way home.

In the meantime, her mother was unable to get to sleep. She had been through several Saturday-night bouts with her husband and daughter, and she sat up reading and watching television. She had been impatient since eleven o'clock, and by midnight she became anxious. After an increasingly frantic hour, she finally had to get some relief and woke her husband out of a deep sleep. She was overcome by anxiety, fear, and guilt. Was this all her fault? Should she have been a firmer mother? Was it too late to remedy the mistakes of the past? What might have happened to the child? Should she have called the people where the party had been, instead of awakening her husband, who hated to be roused in the middle of the night?

The husband immediately launched into an attack against

his wife, daughter, therapists, and analysis in general. This was the result of all the crazy nonsense about analysis, he said, and he would have nothing more to do with any part of it. As his wife, now in tears, asked what this distress had to do with analysis, the husband got angrier. When the wife, in self-defense, accused him of having been an absentee father, he left the bedroom and slammed the door behind him.

Just then, the daughter walked in, accompanied by a young man. Her father took one look, threw the boy out, and pulled his daughter bodily into the living room, demanding to know where she had been. In fear, and genuinely sorry, the girl tried to get away from his grip and started to scream. When she used bad language, her father lost his temper and slapped her cheeks hard.

All this happened so quickly that her mother hardly had time to collect herself. She told the girl to go to bed and assured her that they would talk in the morning. The parents did not get much sleep that night, and there was very little talk in the morning. Instead, the daughter talked to her therapist.

"We had a terrible fight at home," she said to her analyst after she had settled down in the chair and pulled one leg up under her wide skirt, squatting comfortably. "I came home late with Bryan, and my father got so mad he threw him out and beat me up. My mother did not take my side, as usual, and I felt awful."

The analyst, who was not in the girl's home that night, could not be sure what actually happened. If he were a detective investigating a crime, or a judge aiming to learn all the facts, he would have had to hear all sides to establish what, in fact, did happen. However, the analyst is not a detective or a judge, but a therapist, and his job is not to investigate the facts or to make any judgments other than clinical ones, concerned with the pathology of his patient.

He is not so much concerned with what did happen at home, or whether the father did "beat up" the daughter, as with the fact that this is what she is reporting. She is expressing one of her feelings in a certain way. Having seen the girl a few times, he knows by now that she tends to distort reality in several important ways, for definite conscious and unconscious purposes. The analyst wonders what this description really means to his patient. He asks her to tell him more, and as she goes into detail, it becomes quite clear that her father did not "beat her up," but lost his temper and slapped her. Perhaps she needs to make her father look brutal and hostile, possibly because she hopes to arouse sympathy with this kind of distortion. The analyst is attempting to get more evidence from this seeming pattern before he can reach a clinical judgment and ask himself what makes it necessary for this adolescent to seek this kind of sympathy. Would this pattern be applicable only in her relationship to her father, or also to her mother, her teachers, and other significant people, or only to certain figures?

He already knows from previous sessions that the patient unconsciously provokes people into getting mad at her and then proceeds to blame them for being mean. This aspect of her behavior had been visible in several previously reported episodes with fellow students in school and at parties. The patient usually ends up feeling misunderstood and helpless. She is far from being aware that she is contributing toward the hostility directed against her, but before she can recognize such a pattern, the analyst will have to work through several layers of defensive rationalization.

Because the current material pertaining to this topic dealt

with last night's episode, and because the patient is filled with intense feelings about it, the analyst uses this to get more clinical material for the pattern that he senses is becoming visible. He asks her to tell him more about how her father "beat her up," and, following this clarification, he makes a bland comment about her relationship to her father, which he expects will get him more material about the pattern. He says, "You don't get along too well with your father right now, do you?"

Without a moment's hesitation, the patient says, "He's never satisfied." The analyst makes a mental note to the effect that the patient continues to hide behind a now familiar barrier: Not I, but the other fellow, is the aggressor.

She did not have to respond to his comment in this way. There are a great number of possible responses, all of which would tell the analyst something about the personality structure of the patient. She might have said, for example, "I'm not getting along with anybody." This would have suggested an awareness of herself as a common denominator; it would have indicated more insight than her very defensive statement did. If she could have seen that it was not only her father but a great many people with whom she did not get along, it would have been only a short step toward recognizing that something must therefore be the matter with her.

She might have said, "Sometimes we get along all right." This would have suggested a more mature sense of reality, since the analyst knew, from other sessions, that her relationship with her father was quite complex and had many pleasurable aspects to it. That the patient responded as she did presented the analyst with a few immediate tasks. One of the most urgent was to ascertain whether this kind of generalized negativism was still to be considered part of normal adolescent behavior. It did sound like something many an angry teen-ager might say about a parent.

Was this such a remark, or had it more meaning? While the analyst was reflecting on this, the patient continued to talk: ". . . like that Mr. McCormick in school. No matter how hard you study, you can't satisfy him."

And then a sudden break and return to earlier material: "Do you think it is so terrible to come home late once in a while?"

This was, of course, an attempt to play authority against authority, and possibly a repetition of what the girl did at home with her parents—perhaps with her parents and teachers as well. Behind this gambit, some of her uncontrolled impulses could be acted out more uninhibitedly. The analyst had noticed this pattern in previous sessions. He was now trying to establish how much reasonable judgment—that is, not based on guilt or fear—this young patient did, in fact, possess.

He parried the provocation and said, "Isn't your own judgment the important thing here, rather than what I think?"

This made it necessary for the patient to recognize that she was being treated with respect and that her own judgment was needed. She responded favorably by thinking out loud, associating for a few moments: "You mean, what do *I* think . . . I don't exactly know . . . I guess it's not terrible but of course our house is isolated and without a date I sure hate coming home late. . . . I think it's some kind of a battle between my parents . . . who makes the rules . . . I mean I certainly don't have any say in this matter. . . . No, wait a minute, I take that back . . . my mother did ask me what time I thought would be fair. . . ."

"What did you say?"

"Well . . . I said twelve . . . of course I couldn't have said any old time . . . I mean I couldn't have said four in the morning . . . well, no, that really is too late . . . maybe I would say between twelve and two . . . nothing too definite . . . I mean you can't always tell how a party comes off. . . ."

Sensing that the patient was about to go off on more generalized material (the ending of teen-age parties) and away from her own judgment of the role she played in her relationship with other people, the analyst intervened.

"The party probably broke up very late and you came home later than you had planned?" There was a brief silence and her expression suggested that some material was being left out.

"You had a good time with your date on the way home?"

"Naturally. But my father wouldn't like it if he knew it."

This comment was of interest to the analyst, since the girl suddenly connected her father with her adolescent sexual behavior. From what she had previously said, it would have been more realistic if she had referred to her mother, who was openly concerned with petting and necking, while, from all that could be inferred, her father had not made many comments about it. The connection, it seemed, was the patient's and had to do with her own feelings about sexuality and her father. To check on this distinction, the analyst asked a few questions about her father's assumed moralistic position, and got no material to substantiate her statement, "Father would not like it."

There was apparently more to the association, "Father is never satisfied," than could have been known at first glance. Her comment began to sound as if she had tried to satisfy father and, having failed, behaved like a jilted lover, feeling rejected and hostile toward somebody she really loved. Provoking him, as she had done by coming home late, would give her the needed justification or excuse for her hostile feelings, which apparently had deeper roots.

Because some feelings toward parents are often repeated in modified form with other important figures, the analyst wondered whether there was any parallel to the previously mentioned teacher, Mr. McCormick, whom she had also accused of never being satisfied.

It turned out, after some directed questions, that the people whom she could never satisfy were all older men, somehow resembling her father. One possible hypothesis to consider was that she was behaving in this rather self-destructive manner in school and at home to get some response from an otherwise indifferent father: anger was better than no contact. Had she developed this as a pattern and was she failing in school and to some extent at home by unconsciously arranging it?

Again, as with some previous questions, the analyst had to make a distinction between normal adolescent disturbances, temporary pathology, and deeper, unconsciously lodged disturbances. The analyst in this case had to know the many ways in which adolescence usually expresses itself before he could direct his therapeutic efforts toward those aspects of the personality that require deeper probing. He would move very slowly and evaluate each piece of behavior in the complex light of adolescent change. At the same time, he would be more active.

Because in adolescence the core of the personality is threatened by inner and outer demands, the analyst cannot remain as remote as he would in an adult analysis. The adolescent requires more face-to-face contact, and can talk more easily about some things than about others. The patient whom we have just observed would probably consider the analyst not very different from her parents and teachers and would for a long time have great difficulty in talking about her sexual feelings. Whether it is necessary for her to associate at all at this point is an open question, about which there has been a good deal of controversial writing.

As we suggested before, the manner of communication is usually quite different in the analytic therapy of children than it is for adults in a full analysis. This point can be made more clearly if we turn from adolescents to earlier stages of development and observe the ways in which communication takes place with very much younger children.

Because young children often express themselves more directly through play than words, the language of play is frequently used in work with them. It is used for many purposes—to get a better insight into the problems of the child; to help the child express feelings that could not otherwise be discharged; and as a preparatory phase for analytic work with smaller children, similar to the phase described in the case of the aggressive fifteen-year-old boy mentioned before.

Sometimes the language of play is the only one available in the beginning stages of therapy, and illustrates another special characteristic of analytic work with children and young people.

For example, a six-year-old girl was brought to the analyst's office by her mother, who spoke of the child's extreme shyness, her inability to speak according to her age level, her inability to read, dress herself or eat without help, to play alone or with other children.

The mother had been told that Susie was "mentally retarded." This had increased her overprotective attitude and in turn retarded any move toward independence and growth on the child's part. Although Susie sat in the waiting room, crying and clutching her mother's arm, she was willing to take the therapist's hand and walk toward the playroom. The mother was certain a private session with Susie would not work, because the child had not been away from her for a moment since her father's sudden death, two years before.

The death had occurred under tragic circumstances. The family had been on vacation, staying at a small family hotel in the country. Just before Sunday dinner, the mother had gone upstairs, while the father and Susie went for a walk in the garden, where they had played earlier in the morning. The crayon books and crayons were still on the table where they had been left, and Susie, holding her father's hand, was counting tulips in a bed near the garden table. As they straightened up from a close inspection of the flowers and turned to walk toward the table, the father fell to the ground and did not move. He had died of a sudden heart attack.

For a few moments the child was alone with her dead father, until other guests, strolling in the garden, came upon them. The mother, after the initial shock, was sufficiently calm to minister to the child. Susie was told that her father was sleeping, and later that he had gone away. Still later, her mother told her that her father had died, but Susie did not respond to any of these explanations. Her face remained blank, her voice inaudible, her movements greatly restricted. It appeared that since this event, the child had stood still, and had not learned a single new word or number. From the reports of the mother, it appeared that Susie was no different now than she had been two years ago, when she was not yet four years old and had experienced her father's death.

While it was clear from the very start of the therapy that the child got many satisfactions from her mother's concern, it was also obvious that the case was much more complex than could have been imagined. The fact that Susie was able to leave her mother upon first contact with a stranger, the therapist, and walk calmly to the playroom, was outstanding. The therapist left the door open so that the child could see her mother in the waiting room, but when a package was delivered to the door, creating some noise, the therapist asked Susie whether she could close the door for more quiet in the playroom. Without a moment's hesitation, Susie left the crayon book, walked to the door, closed it, and returned to the play table. She continued drawing houses without doors, but with large round windows. The first drawings were very primitive, about on the level of a four-year-old child. Later in the same hour, she began to draw more complicated houses, appropriate for a six- or seven-year-old.

This coexistence of more primitive and more mature behavior was noticeable in all her activities in subsequent sessions. While she kept on with the repetitious question "What's that?", she was able to identify objects accurately and pronounce words clearly. Whenever the therapist did not answer her automatic question—uttered in the voice and tone of a very small child—but looked at her encouragingly, as if to say, "You know the answer to this one," Susie would drop the helpless-infant role and speak in a tone more nearly appropriate to her age. In working with puzzles, Susie would usually begin by putting together pieces that clearly did not connect, and would end by starting another puzzle on the level of her age.

The most startling revelation of her inner development, and her battle against it, came in regard to numbers. Counting had been one of the games she had played with her father, and for several months of treatment, she would persistently call any number of objects "three," which had been her age when she last counted numbers. If her mother or a neighbor gave her a handful of candies and asked her how many there were, Susie would always say three. It made no difference whether one showed her one or ten objects, she always referred to the number as three, almost as though the word "three" were a symbol for all numbers. After several months of therapy, in which she became much more spontaneous and aggressive—including a burst of anger against a Teddy bear she spanked, and demands for more paper—Susie spotted a game of wooden clowns that could be placed on top of each other. She became fascinated by this balancing act, and the therapist, sitting nearby, watched her pile the wooden figures on top of each other. When she had reached the fourth man, the therapist called attention to this fact by saying, "Now we have four, let's try to go higher." Susie, completely engrossed in the rather delicate job of piling the figures higher and higher, counted as she went ahead, and ended by saying with relish, and correctly, "Eight."

At this moment, she glanced at the therapist as though she had given away a very important secret, shook her head, and corrected herself: "I mean three." She had sensed that the therapist was interested in this accomplishment and she denied it, returning to the previous cover-up of semi-retardation. She was, of course, similar to many neurotic children who give up accomplishments when they wish to stay small or punish a parent. Here in miniature is the well-known fear of success, of becoming free from fears, of getting well—a wish that is visible throughout many analyses. It is this unconscious desire to be small, passive, and safe that is the essence of the often confused concept of resistance. In the case of Susie, it is not difficult to understand that fantasies of being with her father could be more easily experienced when she remained stationary at the three-year level at which she had lost him.

As in the analysis of adults, the gains alternated with the backward movements, and some months later, Susie was able to begin kindergarten in the nearby public school. Once enrolled, she reverted to the three-year-old behavior with which she had begun her therapy.

Since the teacher had been helped to understand that it would be better for Susie to take the initiative on her own, rather than be supported in her wish to be small, Susie began to seek out another girl who, like herself, appeared fearful. To the surprise of the teacher, Susie took the leadership with her friend in playing house, a game in which she asked the other girl to play the father. While reporting this in therapy, she sat at the play table putting together a cat puzzle, which she seemingly inadvertently shoved off the edge of the table. She commented, "Poor Pussy fell down," retrieved the pieces, and put the puzzle together again, only to destroy it once more. The next association—for this was what she was expressing—was a question to the therapist about where he lived. Since she had come to see the therapist at his office many times, the question at this point, following both the resurrection of the destroyed cat and the father-mother game in school, seemed significant.

When, later on, she played a similar game with an elephant toy, the meaning became more open. She called the elephant, "Babar," after the children's story, but pronounced it "Papa," and had the toy fall down quite suddenly. She picked it up and then let it fall down, not unlike the game with the cat puzzle. As she was beginning, quite unconsciously, to permit herself to re-experience the death scene, she was also mastering reality by resurrecting the object she cared for. At the same time, she expressed very direct interest in the therapist—first in his residence, and later in his "mother." This was followed by declaring that "My mother is outside, waiting." In a way, she was identifying with the therapist and got enough security from her alliance with him to begin to remember some of the frightening experiences she had kept locked up until now. The energy she had been using to repress painful memories was now freed for constructive activities. Her mother reported that Susie wanted to go to the store and buy her own milk. Her teacher reported that Susie was struggling with writing her name.

When she played again with the wooden clowns, she counted, as before, beyond three, but after five her voice became inaudible. However, this time she did not need to deny her knowledge at the end of the balancing act, and did not declare that the number was "three."

As the very gradual increase of satisfaction in accomplishments progressed, the work with Susie's mother was intensified, for it had become clear that the child's growing independence was not a pure joy to her mother. In some ways, Susie's progress was a threat to her mother, who felt less and less needed as the child began to give up the helpless, infantile role. Only now did the more deep and subtle causes of the child's difficulties begin to appear.

Tragic as the death of her father had been, this was not the major cause of Susie's unconscious refusal to grow. It merely facilitated an already existing tendency. The deeper causes were connected with the child's earliest tie to her mother's unconscious mind and required a careful and gradual analysis of the ways in which the child had developed up to the time her father died. It also required intensive work with the mother, who, like Susie, had until this time denied the real effect on herself of her husband's death. Only when serious physical symptoms forced her to seek attention for herself did she begin to consider herself and her problems as separate from those of her daughter. Until then, she had always declared and sincerely believed that she did not matter at all, that Susie's happiness was the only purpose of her life. Therein was hidden the nucleus of the child's earliest problems.

The direct involvement of the mother is one aspect more typical of work with children than with adolescents. The mother needed therapy for herself, because without it the child's progress would have been that much more difficult.

Another characteristic of therapy for children and young people is the analyst's close contact with significant figures in the child's environment. It is not unusual, as in the case of Susie, for the therapist to make direct contact with the school or with some significant teacher. This is conditioned partly by the fact that referrals to therapy often come directly from the school to the analyst.

The basic goals of analytic therapy with young people, as we suggested at the beginning of this chapter, are the same as in adult analysis. In the case of the fifteen-year-old boy, the goal was not to modify the symptoms. The analyst was not concerned merely with getting the boy to stop his hostile activities, or helping him to study. In the case of the girl, the goal was not better co-operation with her parents, or more mature behavior with boys. In the case of Susie, the issue was not to get her to speak more freely or to act like other children of her age. These accomplishments were by-products and initial gains in the long assault on the deeper underlying neurosis. How the inner conflicts developed and led to the illness might be revealed through a full analysis, which was not attempted in these cases, for the reasons stated at the beginning of the chapter.

SEVEN

·

The Analyst's Training

Psychoanalytic Education in the United States is the title of a recent five-hundred-page book, based on a three-year self-study survey carried out under the auspices of the American Psychoanalytic Association and covering the seventeen training institutes recognized by this group. It goes without saying that if it took the many investigators and contributors to this volume three years and five hundred pages to give a comprehensive picture of the "analyst's training," it will be impossible to do more than sketch a few of the issues in this chapter.

I have selected for discussion, from the many aspects of training, those that seem to be of greatest interest to the general public, based on the questions I have most frequently been asked. There are two main areas of questions that appear to be most on people's minds: The first has to do with the general background of analysts—are they psychiatrists or psychologists; should they have an M.D. or a Ph.D. or any special degree; how and where are they trained for their work? The second area has to do with the so-called different "schools of psychoanalysis."

In this chapter I shall take up only the first issue, and will discuss the second in a later one, on "Other Forms of Psychotherapy." However, it should be emphasized that the first group of questions is not the most significant. Psychoanalysis grew out of the already existing professions of medicine and psychology, and its practitioners have come from both these and other professions. Freud was a medical doctor; his daughter Anna, an outstanding analyst, came from education; other well-known theoreticians were in still other professions. More important than which former profession the analyst comes from is his personal analysis, his theoretical education in the specialized psychoanalytic form of therapy, and the kind of supervision he has had.

There are four items, then, that belong together: (1) preanalytic training, (2) the analyst's personal analysis, (3) theoretical analytic training, and (4) supervision while in training. Let us consider them in order.

Pre-Analytic Training

This is the only truly controversial issue. It has been controversial from the beginning of psychoanalysis, and apparently it will continue to be for some time to come. Ernest Jones, Freud's biographer, in his authoritative history of psychoanalysis, explains why this has come about. Nobody studies to be an analyst, as one studies to be a lawyer or a social worker by completing college and going on to postgraduate school. Therefore, questions have arisen: Should the future analyst first study medicine, specialize in psychiatry, and then go on to analytic training? Since he will not practice medicine but psychoanalysis, does he need the medical background? Wouldn't it be more practical if he first studied psychology or related behavioral sciences and then went on to special analytic training? Why bother with pre-analytic training altogether? Why not emphasize the really significant issues of personal analysis and analytic training?

There have been strong cases for and against each of these points of view, differing with the country and the educational philosophy. Freud himself consistently maintained that pre-analytic training was not significant, that only the candidate's own analysis and special analytic training mattered. He was particularly firm in his position that the study of medicine was not a necessary requirement for the practice of psychoanalysis. He made these views explicit on several occasions, notably in 1925 and again in 1938, toward the end of his life. The 1925 statement was in defense of a nonmedical analyst, Theodor Reik, and was published under the title "The Question of Lay Analysis." In this book, Freud emphasized that "nobody has the right to practice analysis who has not earned this right through thorough training. Whether this person is a physician or not seems to me to be irrelevant." At another point in the same work, he expressed this view even more strongly: "It is unfair and impractical to force a man who wants to cure others of the pain of a phobia or a compulsion neurosis to reach this goal via the detour of a study of medicine."

However, Freud's stand failed to settle the issue of pre-analytic training. Although many people agreed with his position, including a great many analysts today, there are still many more practitioners who insist that medical training is important, if not essential. The reason has to do, at least in part, with the different ways in which psychoanalysis developed in Europe and in this country. Because it originated in Europe, Americans obtained their training at the beginning of the century by "pilgrimages to Vienna and Zurich, and later, in the mid-twenties, to Berlin," in the words of Dr. Robert P. Knight, a former president of the

American Psychoanalytic Association. When these men returned and tried to set up their own training institutes and psychoanalytic clinics, they ran up against the opposition of educational and medical authorities, at first in New York State. This opposition was very understandable because the country was at the time plagued by faith healers and self-styled therapists of various cults. In addition, the authorities were guided by the findings of the now famous Flexner Report, a sharp and most important criticism of medical education in the United States. Written in 1910, it described "a century of reckless overproduction of cheap doctors," and criticized the low level of commercial medical schools, without sufficient scientific knowledge in the curriculum and operated mainly for "pecuniary advantage." The Flexner Report had a profound impact in New York State on the people who granted licenses for schools and clinics, and it is understandable that the psychoanalysts, upon their return from Europe, were told that they could not set up any schools or clinics unless they were affiliated with organized medicine.

This development, which was later paralleled in other states, explains why even today those psychoanalysts who want to belong to an approved psychoanalytic organization have to take the position that the study of medicine is a prerequisite to analytic training, although not all medically trained psychoanalysts accept this position in practice.

This is the background of one school of thought about pre-analytic training—the school that holds that before a man can study psychoanalysis, he has to complete his study of medicine, earn his M.D., specialize in psychiatry, pass the examinations in psychiatry, and become a fully qualified psychiatrist. Only then may he apply to one of the approved training institutes and study the theory and practice of psychoanalysis.

There is another camp that takes a position similar to Freud's on pre-analytic training and maintains that psychoanalysts practice psychotherapy and not medicine, so that the long and costly preparation for medical practice will not, in fact, be used by the practicing psychoanalyst. They believe that a thorough grounding in psychology rather than medicine is much more relevant to the practice of psychoanalysis, and they ask that a future analyst complete his graduate training in psychology, serve his interneship in a hospital, earn his Ph.D., and then go on to analytic training proper.

Both camps agree on one thing—the psychoanalyst practices psychoanalysis, not medicine. Psychoanalysts who have their M.D.s generally consider it against the rules of analysis to prescribe drugs to their analytic patients. The rules of the psychoanalytic situation specifically bar the therapist from physically examining the patient. In practice, therefore, both the medical and nonmedical analyst simply suggest that the patient see a physician when he has physical symptoms, or when organic disturbances are suspected.

If a new patient, for example, reports symptoms that may have an organic basis, the analyst may not be able to take the patient until he has been examined by a physician. I had one such patient. A young woman in her early twenties, referred to me by her college, came for an interview and reported serious disturbances in her ability to concentrate, fears of dying, anxiety about open windows, homosexual disturbances, depression. She was extremely pale and undernourished, and mentioned in passing that she had trouble breathing and suffered from cramps in the heart region. She made light of these physical disturbances and assured me that they were "psychosomatic." She insisted that she had been seeing physicians for years, but on closer questioning it turned out that these examinations had taken place three and four years ago.

In spite of the patient's anxiety, I had to insist that she see a physician and, if he suggested it, a heart specialist. Since she had no physician of her own, I recommended a diagnostician whose judgment I had relied on in the past. When the patient still made light of her physical symptoms, I made it clear that I could not even begin to discuss an analytic schedule with her until we had agreed that the physical symptoms be thoroughly checked. Since she was eager to begin analysis—after years of short-term therapy and college counselling—she did see the recommended physician and the heart specialist. Fortunately, there were no organic findings of any kind, and we could proceed with plans for analytic therapy.

Similar procedures are followed by all responsible analysts, whether the symptoms are reported before or during the process of analysis. Sometimes the physician's recommendations have to be carefully integrated with the analytic therapy. Another patient of mine, a man in his early thirties, worked in the television industry, in a job where his hearing was particularly important in the mixing of sounds. During the second year of his analysis, he complained on several occasions of misunderstanding words and failing to hear certain sounds. Since he was a man who tended to complain easily about the slightest discomfort, I observed this latest symptom for two or three days without doing anything. When the hearing complaint appeared a week later, I suggested that he see an ear specialist for an examination. The specialist saw him, gave him a thorough examination, and reported to me that there was some arrested deficiency in one ear, which was not progressive. He recommended that the patient wear a hearing aid.

I was very concerned about this recommendation because having to wear a hearing aid would have been disastrous to this particular patient. He was an extremely insecure man, overly concerned with his appearance, his grooming, his hair, his clothes. He devoted an excessive amount of energy to appearing casual and "normal," and was terrified lest anybody know that he was in analysis or had anything wrong with him in any way. One day, when he had to wear an eye patch because some dust had irritated his eye, he preferred staying home to going to work. If this man had to wear a permanent hearing aid, he would almost certainly go into a depression, aggravating his suicidal fantasies.

In this case, I conferred with the ear specialist and asked whether the hearing aid was medically absolutely necessary. The doctor assured me that while there was an organic basis for the hearing deficiency, tension could aggravate or diminish it. Since the patient had had the condition for at least fifteen years without any damage to his work, we agreed that I would not tell him about the specialist's recommendation. It became clear that some material which had come to the surface during analysis had increased his tension, which in turn had an effect on the organic problem. When the patient asked about the ear specialist's findings, I told him that the specialist had found an old, arrested condition, which was not progressive but which was aggravated by tension, so that there was no need to worry about the ear. Instead we had to continue from where we had left off—with the process of free association and analysis, which would reduce his many tensions in time. This was very reassuring to the patient, who eventually completed his analysis and had no further hearing difficulties of any consequence to his work.

The same procedure would be followed by the analyst whose pre-analytic training was in the field of medicine. The practice of analysis, therefore, does not help in clarifying the controversy over the best pre-analytic training. However, there is agreement on the necessity of some scientific training before beginning analytic training. In other words, no analyst would propose that anybody can become an analyst so long as he has had his personal analysis. Most would agree that a man must have learned to think scientifically and must have a broad background in the behavioral sciences, as well as a broad cultural background, as preparation for his analytic training. While there is no agreement on what kind of scientific training is necessary, several proposals have been made that attempt to systematize the pre-analytic training issues. Some of these proposals contain detailed outlines for pre-analytic preparation, including graduate study toward a special degree, so that the public can recognize a psychoanalyst by his degree, as it now recognizes a nurse by her R.N. degree. The most practical proposal, in my opinion, has been made by Dr. Lawrence Kubie, who studied the issue of training and, particularly pre-analytic training, for many years. Since this and other proposals apply not only to pre-analytic training but to the preparation for all forms of psychotherapy, they will be discussed in the chapter on other forms of psychotherapy.

Until there is agreement on this and other proposals for the best pre-analytic training, analysts will continue to come from medicine, psychology, social work, and other fields—and will get not only personal analysis but the best possible training and supervision available to them.

The Personal Analysis

If Freud did not manage to settle the controversy over pre-analytic training, he certainly succeeded completely in a more important issue—that the personal analysis of a future psychoanalyst is a basic requirement for training and later practice. He stated this as a recommendation in 1910, and a few years later one of his students enunciated it as a dictum: "No one could any longer learn to practice psychoanalysis without having been analyzed himself." Since this remark, in 1919, the personal analysis of analytic students has become a basic requirement. Today it is the core of psychoanalytic education.

Because the personal analysis of the future analyst is part of his training, it is usually called his "training or preparatory analysis," and the analyst who analyzes the student is called the training analyst. The success or failure of the training analysis rates at least as high or higher than the theoretical-course training, which we shall discuss shortly. It is understood that a future analyst's ability to analyze patients depends to a very high degree on his self-understanding and his ability to attain the high degree of maturity necessary for his future work. The training analysis as part of an educational procedure is probably the only instance where the course of therapy is more significant for the evaluation of a person's ability than his intellectual understanding of theoretical-course content. The average number of hours of analysis for students, as measured in seventeen training institutes over a period of ten years, is about seven hundred hours. At some point during his analysis, the student will begin to take his theoretical training.

The Theoretical Analytic Training

The study of the theory of psychoanalysis began with Freud in the autumn of 1902, when he invited four of his colleagues to his residence in Vienna for a discussion of his work. This little group became known as the Psychological Wednesday Society, continued for seven years, and was then renamed the Vienna Psychoanalytic Society, the name it has retained to the present. Seven years later, in 1909, Freud made his first and only visit to the United States, to give the Stanley Hall Lectures in honor of the president of Clark University, in Worcester, Massachusetts. Although the American Psychoanalytic Association was organized shortly thereafter, in 1911, it was another decade before even informal theoretical training began. Training then was similar to the classic training in the arts, where a master like Leonardo gathered some apprentices around him.

The method of training, a mixture of personal analysis and some control, was called "didactic analysis." It took another ten years before systematic training began. In 1932, the New York Institute of Psychoanalysis was organized, and at the same time similar training institutes were established in other cities.

It may be helpful to remember throughout this discussion on training that methodical instruction in theory and practice is only about thirty years old. This explains in part why the problems of "psychoanalytic education and the university setting have not been solved, but they have been posed and scrutinized with good will and intelligence," as Dr. Bertram Lewin put it in 1957, in a lecture before the American Psychoanalytic Association. The same could be said about psychoanalytic education and hospital settings, but there, too, practitioners are aware of the necessity of more practical solutions.

As might be expected, the development of training methods —course contents, supervision, and controls—did not proceed at an even, steady pace. The International Psychoanalytic Association did not always agree with the American branch; the New York branch differed with institutes in Chicago and Topeka. Each country, each city had its own modification of the main tenets of training. Some institutes concentrated on reading courses and seminars, others on clinical conferences and lecture courses. The course contents differed and the curricula varied considerably. Today, a four-year curriculum is standard procedure in all analytic training centers. If one took a sample of course titles, it would be obvious that all analytic students are studying the specific theory of psychoanalysis, on which all the practical work must rest.

Students are required, for example, to take "Psychoanalytic Ego Psychology," a basic two-year course. Another typical required course is "The Theory of Technique in the Psychoanalytic Process." There may be several seminars on "Dream Interpretation," continuing over one to two years. Courses on "The Theory of Symptom Formation," "Instinct Theory," and "Mechanisms of Defense" are also typical. There may be specialized courses on "The Psychoanalytic Study of Children" or technical courses on "Variations of Technique."

Supervision

While the student is taking these courses, he is also beginning to learn the practice of psychoanalysis. His training institute will assign a patient to him. The student, who has by then studied the theory of the technique, will start to analyze his first patient. Along with this process, he will report weekly to one of his teachers on the course of this first analysis. The teacher, known as the supervisory analyst, is usually not the student's former training analyst.

While the candidate's training analysis was a therapeutic experience, his supervisory analysis is an educational one. Where a candidate has more than one case, he may have several supervisory or control analysts, and he will continue to use analysts for control and supervision for several years following his four-year course.

After the completion of a satisfactory personal training analysis, the four-year curriculum, and several years of supervision of cases, a candidate may or may not be certified by the training institute, which controls the total process. The candidate's analyst, as well as his instructors and supervisors, who are all experienced analysts, have to agree that a candidate can meet the requirements of the profession before he is sent out and allowed to practice on his own.

The training institutes grew out of professional associations, such as the New York Psychoanalytic Society. An accredited candidate will become a member of this or other professional organizations, and it is this affiliation that provides the safeguard for the public, since no specialized degrees are available. The largest association of training centers for psychoanalysts is the American Psychoanalytic Association.

However, there are many qualified analysts who were not trained in these affiliated institutes, and who therefore do not belong to these organizations but to others. These are analysts whose training antedates the formation of training institutes; they may be analysts who preferred to obtain their controls from outstanding analysts of long experience, or analysts who were not eligible for these institutes because of the split in academic-background requirements discussed above. There are analysts who have preferred the original tradition of the Psychological Wednesday Society and have learned the theory of psychoanalysis in small, exclusive study groups. Most of these analysts have also joined together in professional organizations, with rigid membership requirements—subject to verification by the total membership—and with vigilant education committees. Their organizations also provide safeguards for the public. However, they have not always limited their membership to psychoanalysts, but have included other psychotherapists as well. In popular language, some of these organizations represent therapists of the so-called "different schools of analysis." What this term really means will be discussed in the chapter on other forms of psychotherapy.

EIGHT

·

Choosing an Analyst

Except for the population in a few large cities, most Americans don't have the problem of choosing an analyst because the chances are that there will be no analysts to choose from where they live. If they are lucky, there may be one or two in their county. More often there will be one for the whole state. There will be hospitals and county clinics or traveling mental-hygiene units—often excellent services and sometimes not so excellent—but these do not require the complicated business of choosing the right analyst from the many available ones. This problem is very real to people in New York and Los Angeles, Detroit and Chicago, San Francisco and a number of other metropolitan centers.

This chapter, therefore, will be of practical interest only to big-city dwellers, while it may be of academic interest to others. Why the distribution of analysts is so uneven is a complicated question, having to do with community planning, social and economic issues, and a number of other sociological causes that we cannot discuss in the framework of this book. But we might mention in passing some additional factors that have bearing on the glaring inequity between the supply and demand of analytic services.

One is the necessity, inherent in the nature of a field that is continuing to grow and unfold, for close contact with colleagues, for research teams, seminars, workshops. Another is the necessity for continuous supervision and control of cases, a safeguard often maintained by even experienced analysts, who will discuss aspects of a case with several colleagues. Finally, there is what one might call an occupational hazard of analysis.

Because of the role the analyst has to play in the process, he himself does not have the casual social contacts with his patients that the medical practitioner has. He does not, as a rule, leave his office for home calls or frequent hospital visits. Indeed, he rarely faces the patient because of the use of the couch, nor does he have contact with several patients in any one hour. He may face a wall in his office eight or ten hours a day and yet be completely attuned to the associations of his patients. It is a demanding, and in many ways a lonely, situation, which explains why analysts seek to be near colleagues. The necessity for theoretical work, for controls and training of students, and the confining nature of the practice are some of the additional reasons why analysts tend to congregate in one area.

In large cities, where this overconcentration has taken place, the population does indeed face the problem of how to choose the right therapist. Usually people turn to professional or personal sources in this search, and we shall discuss them in this order:

There are a great many professional-referral sources besides the traditional family physician. For many people, the physician is the man who takes care of physical ailments, and they do not always feel free to discuss with him problems other than physical ones, even for a consultation. They may instead turn to their minister or a teacher. Physicians, ministers, and educators are, of course, all objective referral sources who sometimes have contact with the available community psychiatric resources. They are, however, specialists only in their respective fields and cannot always be expected to know what kind of therapy is indicated for a given individual.

Whether a person asks for suggestions or whether somebody else feels called upon to suggest some form of therapy, the more general the referral, the better for the prospective patient. A good, informed professional source would be the family case-work agency that exists in many communities, where there are trained psychiatric social workers with the skill to screen the problems presented and make an intelligent referral to a psychoanalyst, a guidance counsellor, or any number of community services. This has nothing whatever to do with the social or economic status of the prospective patient. Because many family agencies are partially supported by community funds, and because one of their many functions is related to economic problems, a mistaken notion has persisted, until recently, that family agencies are primarily set up to meet the needs of the poor. In reality, the trained family case worker, even in trying to understand the economic problems presented by his clients, is primarily concerned with the psychodynamics of a person who brings an economic problem, a marital problem, a child-guidance situation, or any human conflict to him. Many family case workers have been analyzed— in some of the oldest and best-established agencies, psychoanalysis is practically a prerequisite for employment. They have a realistic concept of what analysis involves, are trained to think diagnostically, and are familiar with psychological-testing services, as well as with the psychoanalytic and other therapies available in the community.

In such a first contact, there is also the element of objectivity, which is necessary in selecting not only the appropriate resource but, within the special field, the practitioner who seems best suited to the patient. This cannot be anything but a suggestion for a first contact: the final choice will be between the analyst and the patient, but there is in such a situation the same workmanlike objectivity—at once interested and detached and confidential—as in a good hospital clinic.

The family case worker is competent to say whether somebody is a qualified psychoanalyst. It may not necessarily be the most scientific competence, but it is much more qualified than the hearsay that is often used as a basis for selecting a therapist. Nevertheless, most people go to a particular analyst because someone they know has recommended him. This has to do with an attitude known as confidence, which is not nearly so self-explanatory as it appears. Nobody has been able to explain satisfactorily just what the term means, but a great many important choices are made on the basis of "confidence." We usually choose physicians and dentists, schools and camps, friends and partners, because we feel that we have confidence in the person or institution. It is the same with analysts or other psychotherapists.

Of course we make all possible inquiries, but, assuming that they turn out satisfactorily, we will probably be willing to accept the suggestion of a friend. In other words, we really choose the therapist partly on the say-so of a friend, or of somebody in whose judgment we have confidence. This somebody is almost as important in our considerations of a choice of therapist as the actual background and personality of the therapist himself.

Let us call this somebody the referral source, for that is what he is, and stop for a moment to consider on which basis our referral source has made his recommendation, and on what experiences his judgment is based. We should probably not pay too much attention to a referral source whose contact with the therapist was second- or third-hand, such as acquaintances who know somebody who is related to a man who was analyzed. This kind of recommendation is too unreliable to have any real meaning.

It is different, of course, if the referral source has had first-hand contact with the therapist and recommends him to friends—a more characteristic situation.

My own experience and informal inquiry among colleagues suggests that former patients frequently become referral sources. In these situations, one should distinguish between people who have finished their analysis and those who are in the middle of it. Patients in the process of analysis sometimes go through phases of enthusiasm for analysis and campaign for this treatment method among their friends. They feel anointed, consider analysis a kind of universal salvation for mankind, and not infrequently scare people away from ever considering such help. Other patients, during troublesome phases of their analysis, have very little to say for either analysis or their analyst. Depending on the different phases of treatment they are in, they may be very sympathetic or very angry at the analyst and, in discussing the subject with their friends, report according to their temporary mood. It is wise to remain skeptical about both the enthusiasm and the hostility of patients in the middle of analysis.

People who have finished analysis can be more objective. However, while it is helpful to know well somebody who has had a successful analysis, one should not assume that this friend's former analyst is necessarily the best choice for oneself. Unless one knows a good deal about the objective judgment of the referral source, one cannot evaluate his recommendation very easily. The same is true of people who have finished analysis and feel that it was a bad experience. Neither positive nor negative responses necessarily enable one to draw too many conclusions about the qualifications of the analyst.

One of the reasons for this is that most people do not have the opportunity to know somebody equally well both before and after his analysis. If we could see the difference in his personality by comparing the two states, it would be easier to draw conclusions about his analytic experience. Often we meet somebody we do not consider very well adjusted and, upon learning that he has been analyzed, wonder what kind of experience he had. We should also ask what he was like before his analysis. Yet this is something one is usually not inclined to do, as one personal experience, in which I reacted the way many people would react, showed.

I met a man during my vacation who struck me as particularly maladjusted and difficult to get on with socially. He dressed oddly and behaved in such a peculiar manner that he was termed the oddball by the small resort community. People tried to avoid him in the dining hall, on the lake, by the benches.

While I was sunning myself one afternoon, he sat down next to me and began to talk about himself as if he had known me for years. Being a captive audience, I was forced to listen. In chatting about work, he learned what my profession was and promptly informed me that he had been in analysis. Knowing that the term "analysis" is used loosely by many people, I assumed that he did not mean real psychoanalysis but perhaps some brief psychotherapy or counselling of a supportive nature. However, he insisted on going into detail about his therapeutic experience and soon convinced me that he had gone through at least the motions of an analysis. It was very difficult to know just what had taken place in this analysis, and I wondered about the therapist who had conducted it.

This was my only contact with the man and I could not really form any opinion about his analysis, but when, some time later, I heard someone mention the name of his analyst, I experienced a brief moment of conflict. Without at first knowing why, I suffered a sensation of discomfort on hearing his name. I realized that I was having an irrational reaction to one patient of this analyst, and that I had no business making any kind of judgment on such a basis.

Nevertheless, this somewhat prejudiced reaction would, I am afraid, have remained with me had I not by chance talked to a colleague who happened to visit the same resort the following year. In reminiscing about the place and the people, my colleague mentioned the man's name, and it turned out that he had seen him once for a consultation but because he had had no time to take him on for treatment, he referred the patient to his future analyst. When I spoke of my puzzled reaction to this man, my colleague was surprised. In his opinion, the man had made an excellent recovery, judging by the state he had been in five years before. My friend described his condition then, his years of struggle with illness in several hospitals and, prior to analysis, with drugs, and suggested that his analyst had done a remarkable job with a very sick man.

This unusual bit of luck made it possible for me to correct my naïve impression and get more perspective, but if this kind of thing can happen to someone who is working in the field, no wonder people in general draw conclusions about an analyst from the state in which they find his former patients. In other words, one must take care when one gets recommendations from former patients or from friends of former patients, particularly when the analysis has not been completely successful (or when we feel that it has not been). When a former patient reports positively about his experience, there is no reason why we may not want to consider this person's former therapist.

The whole matter of developing confidence and trust begins in early childhood. It has conscious as well as unconscious aspects that play an important part in the confidence one has in the referral source. But there are many rational and objective causes for having confidence in somebody's judgment. We may actually have experienced the ways in which a friend has been helpful, has used good judgment in difficult situations, and has proved reliable—not by his words but by his actions. We may have found that this has been a thoughtful and sensitive friend, who is able to care about somebody else and does not expect his advice to be followed simply because he says so. If we can ask this friend for the facts about a recommended therapist, we are checking on the basis both of our friend's judgment and of the therapist. The reliable and responsible referral source will not only *not* be insulted by our probing questions, he will welcome intelligent inquiry. Only if the friend has made his recommendation without much factual knowledge will he resent questions.

We can begin our factual inquiry about the analyst and his professional organizations with the referral source. We discussed in the previous chapter some of the significant aspects of an analyst's qualifications. This, however, still does not tell us much about the analyst's competence, his talent, his artistry. Another way of saying this might be, "How can I make sure that this analyst—who is technically qualified—is the right person for me?" The transposition highlights the subjective factor involved in any choice and, with it, the law of chance and margin for error. Perhaps it might be made more explicit—there is absolutely no sure way to guarantee that the analyst chosen is precisely the best one for a certain individual. Given the standard qualifications—his analysis, his theoretical training, his control and supervision, his membership in certain professional societies—given these minimum, factual requirements, the question of his particular personality and how it is suited to the particular patient will, in the end, be the determining factors. Some excellently trained practitioners do not have as much success with their patients as their qualifications would suggest, because they may be more gifted in theoretical understanding than in practical application. They make fine

research workers, but not necessarily the most creative practitioners. On the other side, there are practitioners whose theoretical
contributions are insignificant, while their day-by-day work with
patients is superb. The spark of an exceptional gift is significant
in the consideration of analysts, as it is with practitioners in any
field of human endeavor.

Before discussing some of these qualities, it is necessary to
make one point quite clear. Even the most excellent analyst is in
no case the ideal parent—whom nobody has ever had, yet many
people continue to search for—nor does he have special human
qualities that make him in any way superior to his patients or to
people in other fields of work. Analysts have their own troubles,
just as their patients do, and though they have been analyzed and
trained, they may not have necessarily solved all their problems
for all time. Two kinds of myths persist about analysts or therapists. One is that analysts' personal adjustments are notoriously
poor, that they have more divorces and more maladjusted children
than other people; the other is the opposite, that analysts live
thoroughly well-run lives with no clouds to mar the bliss and
peace in which their homes and offices are enshrined.

These myths parallel the black-and-white kind of thinking
that one finds in phases of childhood about parental figures—
either parents are utterly terrible or they are incredibly wonderful. It is as impossible to make any kind of generalizations about
the personalities of analysts as it is to make sound generalizations
about the personalities of lawyers, physicians, plumbers, or jour-
nalists. There are no resemblances in appearance, character, manner, or personality among analysts, or among people in any
profession or trade. The only things analysts have in common are
their training and background in analysis, just as the only thing
lawyers have in common is the fact that they have gone to law
school. The speculations about character similarities or the "kind

of mind" that people who go into certain professions are said to have are spurious and cannot be well documented by any stretch of the rational imagination.

If there were recognizable traits for analysts, training schools would not have had to spend years of research trying to determine criteria for the acceptability of candidates. As a matter of fact, people in the field, who are interested in selecting the most gifted applicants, do not really know which applicant will in the end make a good practitioner. Not only can they tell nothing from the applicant's appearance, general and educational background, interviews, and opinions of teachers and colleagues—they do not even know much after having given all the known personality tests. There are certain personality traits that seem to be more desirable than others in prospective therapists, but none of these forms the basis for a generalization about the "type" that makes a good analyst. If this is true—and there seems no doubt about the lack of scientific criteria for selecting candidates—what could possibly be the basis for the popular generalizations about analysts or therapists in general? Why should the children of analysts, for example, be different from any other children? What is probably often confused is the fact that analysis is a certain parent's job, just as teaching is another man's job. Why should one assume that analysts' wives or children are better or worse or different from others? Physicians' children are not any healthier than other children, nor are teachers' children necessarily better students.

The only generalizations one can make about the personality of a man and his work have to do directly with the nature of his work. One has the right to assume that a musician has a good ear, or that a dancer has body control. This is a long cry from assuming that all musicians take dope or that all dancers are homosexual.

What occupational generalizations could one make about analysts? It would be reasonable to assume that a good analyst, who has had some years of experience, has had to become modest in his attitude toward his patients, because he has discovered the never-ending complexity and intricacy of the human psyche. This humbleness, which one should be able to find in a good analyst, is not the result of his noble soul, but of having treated sick people for a long time and, in the process, discovered what a tough job it is and how little one knows. In other words, the modesty or reflective thoughtfulness is the result of having worked with people intensively. The analyst's modesty is the result of his work, just as the luminous, penetrating eye of a sea captain comes of having scanned the horizon for many years, through fog and sun.

There are other by-products of having analyzed people for some time, which, again, are not innate qualities but the results of the work. Besides real modesty, a good analyst will have had to become a warm human being with an inner readiness to understand and to care. Unless he has developed these qualities, he cannot follow his patients' associations with both intuition and scientific knowledge, day after day. A good analyst will have had to remain extremely alert and flexible to new experiences, in learning from his patients and their experiences. The analyst who has succeeded over a period of time cannot possibly remain a know-it-all, even if he had this tendency in his personality to begin with. Learning from patients is necessary because of the distinct nature of each patient and the individuality of each experience.

The individuality of each and every experience may be illustrated by a simple example. A male patient reported that his girl friend was reluctant to enter into intimate sexual relations with him. He reacted to this by telling her, "I can wait." Do we know what he meant by this statement? If we assume we do, we will fail to understand the man. His girl friend, for reasons of her own vanity, assumed that he implied she was so desirable that he could wait until she was ready. Another interpretation might be that he would wear her out by giving her enough rope. The statement could mean, "There is no hurry." Or it could mean, "I don't care that much." And it could mean many more things.

In the case of this patient, it meant something else. This particular patient had always felt impelled to seduce women, yet was reluctant to have sexual intercourse, because he experienced extreme anxiety and frequently became impotent before the climax was reached. In his case, the statement "I can wait" really meant, "I'd rather wait indefinitely and play seductive games and avoid intercourse altogether."

One could not learn the meaning of this seemingly obvious statement unless one were constantly aware of the individuality of each expression and each experience. One cannot assume anything, and one must maintain a learning attitude constantly. The experienced analyst knows he has to learn continuously from his patients in order to decipher the deeper meaning of what they say. The matter is, of course, much more complicated than this little example would suggest, because beyond the multiple meanings of a statement, made consciously, are many layers of preconscious and unconscious meanings, which have to be seen in connection with the visible content of any association.

The other aspect of the learning experience lies in the necessity of understanding the total human being behind the clinical material that he presents. People are frequently under the impression that the analyst tries to fit his patient into a given theoretical frame. This is a misunderstanding or an oversimplification. The theory of psychoanalysis, like all theories, is by definition a generalization. In the natural sciences, the generalizations can lead to definite laws because variables can be controlled and the results predicted. It is possible to predict accurately the amount of time it will take a given weight to fall to the ground from a given height. The weight can be duplicated, the level of height can be duplicated, the air current can be eliminated in a vacuum—all the factors can be controlled, and the experiment can be repeated with predictable results. In the social sciences, many variables can be predicted and controlled, but the individuality of each human being is a variable that defies all exact prediction. Since no two organisms, no two psychical structures, are alike, it is never possible accurately to duplicate experiences or to predict behavior.

As long as the social sciences deal with large groups, some generalizations can be made, but as soon as it comes to understanding individuals, theory cannot provide a blueprint for action, but only a broad framework. Absolute laws are not possible in understanding individuals. One can say, for example, that infants who are separated from a mothering figure in the first two months of life will experience feelings of deprivation. But how they will cope with this deprivation cannot be predicted. Whether they will compensate for it with increased aggression, or succumb to it with massive withdrawal, cannot be learned from the theory, but will require clinical observation in minute detail. It is this process of following the individual development in detail that distinguishes the practitioner from the theoretician.

The first-rate practitioner cannot possibly be arrogant or make himself out to be a magician who can read another person's mind. He will have had to develop a healthy respect for the intractability of many character structures. He will have had to develop a certain simplicity from the compassionate neutrality that is one of the necessary attitudes in this work. He will have to possess a good deal of warmth and some humor in order to maintain the necessary balance in the face of so much tension in his patients, hour after hour. These qualities will come across to a patient in the first interview. They are not reflected in the framed diplomas of academic degrees or in the number of professional affiliations listed in membership directories, but they may provide additional safeguards in the search for the right therapist.

To some people, the task of choosing an analyst may seem overwhelming, because we have emphasized the difficulties and advised caution in the choice. Actually, the choice of an analyst is not as difficult or as discouraging as I may have made it seem. Essentially, what I have said is that professional referral sources are better than private ones, but this is no more than a suggestion. It is perfectly natural to recommend somebody with whom one has had a good experience, and in practice many people have had interviews with several analysts before starting analytic work.

NINE

·

Other Forms of Psychotherapy

This chapter is something of a departure from the main theme of
the book. Until now, we have talked about only one form of
psychotherapy—the one developed by Freud and named by him
"psychoanalysis." We have limited our discussion to psychoanalysis as one form of the treatment of mental illness. Even within
this limitation, I have had to leave out discussion of theory and
technical aspects. I have merely answered some of the popular
questions asked about psychoanalysis.

How then, one may ask, can we cover the many other forms
of psychotherapy in one brief chapter? The answer is that one
cannot really begin even to outline the theoretical and practical
aspects of other forms of psychotherapy. Each of them, with its
particular theory, methodology, and applicability, requires a full-
length book. No attempt will be made to do justice to this task.
Some accounts of other schools of therapy have been written, and
there are references to them at the end of this book.

Then why mention the other forms of therapy at all in the
context of this book? I have asked this question of myself many
times and wished that I could leave this chapter out altogether.

The reason it had to be written is the current confusion that exists about the so-called "schools of psychoanalysis."

This chapter was written not to clarify in any detail other forms of therapy but to distinguish them from psychoanalysis and thereby continue with the original task—to clear up misconceptions about this one form of treatment.

For many reasons, some therapists who had worked closely with Freud broke away and developed very different theories of therapy, but retained the name of Freud's treatment method. Of course, Freud could not restrain anybody from using the name of his treatment method for their own method, even though he objected to it in one of his rare polemical pieces, written in 1914—his "History of the Psychoanalytic Movement." In it he stated that he thought he was qualified to know what psychoanalysis is and what it is not, but by then his method had become famous, and people were well aware of the prestige connected with its use. The various therapists had given new names to their various forms of therapy, but the differences were glossed over in popular language, so that today many people use the term "psychoanalysis" in a generic sense, as though it were synonymous with psychotherapy. Strictly speaking, the term "schools of psychoanalysis" is not really meaningful, any more than "schools of the relativity theory" would be. There are, rather, schools of psychotherapy. If some of the other major forms of therapy are listed briefly here, it is done out of fairness to both psychoanalysis and the many other therapies, which have the right to their independent existence but should not, through misleading labels, be confused with analysis.

One of the first therapists to work with Freud in the Psychological Wednesday Society, who found himself more and more in theoretical disagreement with Freud, was Carl Gustav Jung. A Swiss psychiatrist, Jung separated himself increasingly from Freud's theories, and by 1912 had established his own school of psychotherapy, known as the school of Analytical Psychology. This school, with headquarters in Zurich, has been of particular interest to students of cultural history and mythology. Jung's studies of primitive mythology and art forms have influenced these fields. Earlier, some of his theoretical concepts found their way into popular language, and his terms "introvert" and "extrovert" are still as much a part of the popular language as his word-association tests are of psychological testing.

Jung's theoretical conception of the human personality differed from Freud's in significant areas. His emphasis was on what Jung called the "collective unconscious," by which he meant "powerful psychological trends rooted in man's biological equipment." He emphasized what he called the "racial past" and his use of such terms as "symbol" was very different from Freud's. To Jung, a symbol is "the best possible formulation of a relatively unknown thing which cannot conceivably, therefore, be more clearly or characteristically represented." His theory stresses symbolism and certain aspects of religion as being especially significant to people in middle life and after. Since he did not conceive of the importance of infantile, instinctual life, his view of neurosis and psychosis differed sharply from Freud's and did not accept the concept of repression. It follows that, in Jung's form of psychotherapy, reliving is not necessary, since Jung did not accept the return of what has been repressed as one of the origins of neurosis. Since this is one of the basic characteristics of psychoanalysis, it does not clarify things to speak of "Jungian psychoanalysis." Instead, it should be recognized that there is a school of psychological thought, created by Jung, which practices its special form of psychotherapy.

Another original member of the Psychological Wednesday Society who broke away from Freud and established his own school was Alfred Adler. His is known as the school of Individual

Psychology. He himself made it clear that his form of therapy was not psychoanalysis but therapy in which education and encouragement play a much larger part than exploration. He repudiated most of Freud's basic theoretical ideas and seldom used such a basic concept as the unconscious. (When Adler referred to the unconscious, he understood it differently from Freud.) Since he wrote and spoke a great deal, he was known to many people—teachers, physicians, criminologists, the general public. His terms "inferiority complex" and "superiority complex" have understandably become widely known, since most people in our society are familiar with both feelings. In his concept of child development, he distinguished what he considered some outstanding "types," such as the oldest or the youngest child, the spoiled or the hated child. He emphasized in his theories what he called "organ inferiority" and compensation for bodily defects, so that, for example, he gave much weight to the fact that Demosthenes, the great orator, had early been afflicted by a speech handicap. Adler's followers attempt to give the discouraged patient an "exercise in co-operation," as one of his students put it.

Karen Horney, who followed the psychoanalytic method until late in her life, emphasized adaptation to life situations, in ways similar to Adler. As she put it, "The formulation I have sketched . . . puts the environment and its perplexities into the center. . . ." For example, she did not deny the biological importance of sexual drives, but explained neurotic sexual difficulties by the value placed upon them socially, rather than by their biological urgency. She, too, repudiated Freud's theories about the instincts. She, too, emphasized personality types, such as "aggressive types" or "compliant types," and viewed neurosis as a deviation from the "human potential." In her theories, Dr. Horney stressed the conflicts inherent in social values. It was her belief that the contradictions of our society—such as competition and co-operation—most affect those people who are most dependent on the society's approval; they often become ill because they cannot reconcile these conflicting trends. Her school of therapy is called the Association for the Advancement of Psychoanalysis, even though her theories of "basic anxiety" and neurosis, her emphasis on "cultural factors," and her treatment methods are basically different from psychoanalysis as developed by Freud.

The emphasis on environment as a major source of human conflict is characteristic of a number of schools of therapy, not all of which were ever affiliated with Freud or his method of therapy.

The American psychiatrist Harry Stack Sullivan, in particular, who was trained by Dr. William Alanson White and who founded a psychiatric foundation named after Dr. White, established his own school of therapy, which is known as the school of Interpersonal Relations. Because of its original location in the nation's capital, it is also known as the Washington School. In Sullivan's therapy, the focus is not so much on the individual per se and his instinctual drives as on the interpersonal aspects of his life situation. Sullivan's theoretical concept of the personality and how it developed is basically different from Freud's. Since Sullivan considers the interaction between an organism and its environment as "all-pervasive," he objects in principle to the idea of organized impulses, or drives that can be sharply distinguished. His concepts of the "self" and his interpretation of "symbols" are specific to his school of thought and differ from Freud, Jung, and, to some degree, from Adler and Horney. He stressed the idea of the adaptability of the human being, but, like Adler and Horney, Sullivan thought in terms of types of personalities, which he called "diagnostic syndromes," such as the self-absorbed type, the incorrigible type, the negativistic type.

Sullivan was also influenced by the findings of anthropology and sociology, and invented several new terms for his theoretical concepts, which require special study. (The same is true for the theories of Kardiner, Rogers, and others.) If Sullivan, for example, speaks of the "power motive," this is not at all the same as Adler's "power drive."

All these different schools of therapy have their own highly developed theoretical structures, their own implementations of theory and practice, and their own separate training institutes.

In addition to these defined forms of therapy, there are many individual psychotherapists who cannot be labeled as belonging to any one school of thought but who have adopted aspects of one school and developed it through their own scientific efforts, or who have used what they consider the most valid theories from a number of different schools. These therapists represent what they would call an eclectic view of psychotherapy, and practice their own individual forms of treatment.

Depending on a therapist's individual orientation, his techniques of treatment vary greatly. Some therapists do not use free association, while others employ a modified form of this kind of communication. The therapist's role also varies, depending on his theoretical orientation. Where the aim is more educational than exploratory—as in psychoanalysis—the therapist attempts to provide useful learning experiences for the patient. Other therapists go beyond this, and help the patient with active advice and guidance. Their relationships to their patients differ, according to their therapeutic aim. In psychoanalysis the therapist is an anonymous figure, but some practitioners of other types of psychotherapy so disagree with this concept that they may engage in social relationships with their patients, make contact with the patients' families, and become a kind of family friend and adviser.

Therapists also differ in the intensity and length of treatment they provide. Some aim only at alleviating painful symptoms through short, intensive psychotherapeutic counselling.

For some forms of maladjustment, individual therapy has been found to be ineffective, while treatment in groups has proved more successful. In recent years, group therapy has developed into a special form of therapy, made particularly popular through wide application at first in the Army and in hospitals, and later adopted by private practitioners. Today the practice of therapy in groups has a special literature of its own, and specialized professional associations with their own training requirements. According to some of the spokesmen for group therapy, the group is considered a "new permissive family" for each of the patients, in which the tolerant climate and the objective view of the group therapist enable the members to give and take spontaneously. Sometimes patients in group therapy also have individual sessions with the therapist, known as combined therapy. Like many of the other therapies, group therapy is educational in nature, and attempts to re-educate the parts of the personality that did not develop in the past. It is often used with people who have had common experiences, such as groups of mothers of young children or, particularly, groups of adolescents who have banded together against society. With certain forms of juvenile delinquency, group therapy has often proved more effective than individual treatment.

One of its key aspects and its special values derive from the fact that a number of people interact in the presence of a single trained professional leader. The leader is not only not anonymous, as in analysis, but freely offers observations, guidance, and suggestions. This factor, as well as the presence of other people, marks this form of therapy as a unique treatment method not to be confused with psychoanalysis. Terms such as "group psychoanalysis" are inaccurate descriptions of both group therapy and psychoanalysis.

Other therapists may aim at readjustments through pure suggestion, or, if they have a medical background, through hypnosis or drugs. This points up the fact that psychotherapists in general, like psychoanalysts, may have a variety of backgrounds. However, psychotherapy, as a general term, is less clearly defined than psychoanalysis. In fact, there is still a question as to what psychotherapy actually is, how it can be defined, and who is qualified to practice it. Of course, there are many definitions, but no single one that is accepted by everybody and that has universal legal recognition—a state of affairs that has left the field open to quacks and poorly prepared therapists.

Questionable practices have led to a concerted effort by the responsible organizations of psychotherapists to get uniform, legal standards for their profession. To achieve this end, educators, legislators, psychiatrists, physicians, social workers, and psychologists—all of them concerned with the protection of the public—have met in the last few years, in a number of state capitals, to discuss with their state governments ways and means of improving the chaotic situation.

Some professions, notably psychologists, have succeeded in obtaining certification from some state legislatures, which restrict the use of the title "psychologist" to those who have passed stringent admission tests. This has legalized psychological services of many kinds, including psychotherapy, in those states—for example, New York—where the State Commissioner of Education has made such rulings. Within the meaning of the Education Law in New York State, psychotherapy is defined as "the use of verbal methods . . . with the intent of assisting a person . . . to modify attitudes and behavior which are . . . emotionally maladaptive." This definition of psychotherapy is broad and applies only to certified psychologists in New York State. However, people who are not certified psychologists may still hold themselves to be psychotherapists.

Since the concept of psychotherapy has not yet been universally defined, it has been applied to many forms of help. Whether various forms of counselling or child guidance should be included under the heading of psychotherapy is a matter of judgment. Certainly there are workers in these fields who would define their activity in this way. Some of them come from medicine, others from social work, still others from education or the ministry. Psychiatric social workers in private practice, marriage counsellors, and pastoral psychologists all consider their work therapeutic in nature. Some call it psychotherapy. Others hesitate to describe it in this way, but at the present time they have as much right to call it psychotherapy as anyone else.

The most generally accepted methods of professional training for this insufficiently defined field are in hospitals often affiliated with universities. Residents in psychiatry and internes in psychology receive practical training in the treatment of mental illness, in addition to the theoretical instruction given in university classes. The psychological interne is frequently concerned with administering psychodiagnostic tests, but part of his training includes the practice of psychotherapy.

The psychiatric ward in a hospital gives the students broad experience with psychotic patients, but relatively little opportunity to study neurosis, except in the outpatient or mental-hygiene clinics that are sometimes affiliated with hospitals. However, once the psychiatrists and psychologists have served their training, they often set up private practices where, contrary to their hospital experience, they have to treat many forms of neurosis. It is therefore understandable that many young psychiatrists and psychologists attempt to get more training in the treatment of the neuroses and apply to psychoanalytic training institutes, or other training centers. For the reasons given in Chapter VII, they do not always succeed in getting this specialized education.

Thus the question of training for psychotherapy in general

presents many unsolved problems, just as the issue of pre-analytic training does. The two issues are, in fact, closely related by the one factor that has not been mentioned so far in this book— the very real need for many more and better psychotherapeutic services.

Whether one looks at the controversy over the pre-analytic training of psychoanalysts or at the fact that psychiatrists and psychologists in general need more training in the treatment of neuroses, or whether one chooses to be concerned with the question of who is best qualified to practice psychotherapy at all, the one overriding issue is the enormous gap between supply and demand in the mental-health services of this country.

Mental illness is Public Enemy No. 1, and the prevention and treatment of this mass disease should constitute our first line of national defense. It does not mean too much to most people to read statistics—nine million psychoses, or four million alcoholics, or one divorce for every four marriages (1960 figures), as against the twelve thousand psychiatrists, five thousand clinical psychologists, and a few thousand psychotherapists of various orientations spread over the vastness of our country. But it is clear that a great many more psychotherapists, psychoanalysts, psychiatric social workers, and other mental-health workers are needed if we are even to begin to meet the need.

People who have thought about both the needs of the population and the training problems are suggesting that these two questions be considered together. It is possible, some experts suggest, to solve the problem of what background future analysts should have and what training future psychotherapists in general should have, and at the same time to increase the army of mental-hygiene workers. Of the many proposals made, the one by Dr. Lawrence Kubie, who has long studied the problem of training in the light of the national problem, seems to be the most inclusive. Briefly,

Dr. Kubie is suggesting the creation of a new profession—a doctor of medical psychology, "trained in medical schools and teaching hospitals jointly with academic university departments in a co-ordinated curriculum compounded of all of those disciplines which are important to an understanding of the mind and heart of man, both in illness and in health."

The highlights of the Kubie proposal are a seven- or eight-year educational program, including the basic medical sciences (as studied now by those who plan to do research, not practice medicine), combined with the essentials of clinical psychology; hospital experience as a psychological interne, combined with experience as a medical social worker, among organic and later psychiatric illnesses; a personal analysis after some years of advanced training and experience in therapy for the neuroses, followed by the standard psychoanalytic courses. This would lead to a comprehensive examination and a license permitting the practice of psychotherapy under the degree of Doctor of Medical Psychology. Dr. Kubie envisions the passage of a Psychological Practices Act, paralleling the existing Medical Practices Act.

In the meantime, the many forms of psychotherapy, with their different training methods, will continue, as therapists, educators, and legislators work to evolve sound and uniform standards for the whole field of psychotherapy. And the people most concerned with better protection of the public against unsound and unethical practices are the psychotherapists themselves, as the membership requirements of their professional organizations indicate. These organizations check the academic background and psychotherapeutic training of applicants before admitting them to membership, and take responsibility for their professional conduct. Because of the many schools of psychotherapy, there are more professional associations than can be listed here. However, a few references can be found at the end of this book.

The many professional organizations, different schools of psychotherapy, and variety of practices are also indications of continuous growth in the field and of the need for many different services. Aside from the fact that many more therapists are needed, there is the economic factor; some forms of psychotherapy are so expensive that a large number of people cannot afford them. And some of the forms of therapy that have developed are meeting some of the problem where psychoanalysis cannot—by shortening the process of therapy, working with groups, and so on. This is not the only, or even the major, reason for these forms of therapy; nonetheless, they have made some services available to people who otherwise would go without any therapy. It is a sad truth that the one outstanding form of psychotherapy particularly suited to the treatment of neuroses remains too expensive for the majority of the population.

TEN

·

Analysis for the Middle Class?

A schoolteacher in his early thirties, pleasant and attractive, found himself unable to form any meaningful relationships with women. While he wanted nothing more than to get married and raise a family, he grew increasingly frightened of the prospect as he got more involved with a young woman. The fright affected his sleep and his work in the classroom. He began to look pale, went to the doctor in his town, and was given a clean bill of health. He was told that organically there was nothing wrong with him. The doctor gave him some tranquilizers, and told him to take it easy and rest as much as possible.

The teacher then found reasons to break off his romance, and felt better for a short time. However, he now found himself sluggish and irritated with everybody. Nothing interested him very much, and he went about his job in a haphazard fashion until his supervisors began to wonder about him. Colleagues said he had no fun in life. His family said that he needed to get married.

When he went to parties or picnics, he always found himself attracted to some young women, but, knowing his pattern from years of bitter experience, he was afraid to try again, and stayed away from dating or any involvements that could lead to the one thing he wanted most and was most afraid of—marriage.

One day, after class, one of his students asked to see him for some help with a mathematics problem. The teacher spent an hour with the girl and, to his horror, discovered that he was becoming excited by her. He noted, in reflecting about the incident later, that he had inadvertently kept his hand near her arm while holding the book; he was aware that he had had fantasies about her body. His voice had become husky, his mouth dry. He had held the door open for her, as if they had had a date, and had kept staring after her as she walked away from the school. His excitement was intense, he was extremely uncomfortable, and he realized how close he had come to being a real danger to himself, to the school, and to the community. All of a sudden, it hit him that there really was something wrong with him and that he had to do something about it.

After considerable time and very understandable hesitation, he confided in a colleague who did guidance work in a nearby school. The colleague was friendly and sympathetic, and suggested the name of an analyst in the nearest city. The teacher found himself in deeper conflict than before, because he was aware of the financial problems ahead of him if he were to embark on a treatment method as prolonged and expensive as psychoanalysis. In order to avoid this costly step, he considered some other possibilities first. He made an appointment with his minister, who was well known for his wisdom in counselling and had considerable knowledge of pastoral psychology. After two sessions with the minister, it was clear that more was needed than pastoral counselling.

The teacher followed the minister's advice and spent a few months in the local family-counselling service, but the psychiatric social worker, like the minister, had to tell him that what he really needed was psychoanalysis; his problems were greater than the conscious mind could handle. His fears were below the level of reasoning, outside the range of advice—indeed, they had deep roots in the unconscious part of his mind and reached far back to the very earliest experiences in his infancy. While the sessions with his minister and the family-counselling service had been very helpful to him, in the sense that they had enabled him to talk freely about his predicament, the deeper levels of his trouble remained untouched.

Finally, he made an appointment with the analyst and took the train to the city for his first appointment. The analyst made it easy for him to talk; he helped him to say things that were difficult, aided him over awkward pauses, demanded no continuity, let him go from past to present and back to the past, was not shocked by his fantasies or his sexual feelings toward the student. It was a good first interview, and the teacher felt immeasurably relieved. The hour was nearly up before he realized it, and a few practical things had still to be settled—the time of the appointments, the frequency of sessions, the analytic fee.

At this point, the teacher encountered the major obstacle of the middle-class patient after he has conquered the hurdle of how to choose an analyst: How was he to pay for a full analysis? The analyst did not have any hours free just then, but was able to offer some in the coming autumn. He explained to the patient that he should see him four times a week; he reduced his fee to twenty dollars an hour and ventured the guess that this process might last as long as four years.

The young teacher went back to the station in a state of bewilderment and cold fury. A detail like the eighty-cent train fare between home and the city stayed with him—the train fare alone would be a few hundred dollars a year. If this went on for four years, was he going to spend a thousand dollars on transportation? Wasn't this a crazy idea, when his yearly salary was around seven thousand before taxes?

In the train, he took pencil and paper and tried to be calm while he figured out the expense of this much-heralded analysis. What was he going to let himself in for? At the rate of twenty dollars an hour—and he had to laugh when he remembered this was a reduced fee—it would amount to something like four thousand dollars a year. His rent was about a thousand with light and gas. Even if the analysis were deductible as a medical expense, his taxes would still run close to a thousand dollars. What about food, clothes, insurance, pension plan, telephone, contribution to his mother, not to mention a newspaper, cigarettes, or a movie?

This was obviously a mad fantasy, something that ordinary people like himself should not even think about. What had he even gone there for in the first place? Why this absolute waste of time?

The teacher felt trapped. He knew by now that he had some very real problems, which, if untreated, could cause him and others serious damage. He had attempted to do something about them by inexpensive methods and had been told that more was needed; after seeing the man who could help him, he had had to recognize that this method of treatment was not for him. He was ready to accept psychoanalysis as the method of treatment, he had no questions about the qualifications of the analyst, but he was in no position to make use of it.

This young teacher is representative of a very substantial section of the population that is in need of analysis and cannot afford it. He is representative on more than personal grounds. His day-by-day work puts him in close contact with people—particularly young people—so that a resolution of his unconscious problems is of particular importance. A man like this teacher might get into trouble without the right kind of help. Once he has committed a crime, society will spend thousands of dollars to apprehend and prosecute him and several thousand dollars more to keep him alive in a state institution, hospital, or prison. But at the point where he might be helped, there is not a cent for him in any local, state, or federal budget.

What is the answer, short of a full analysis? What does a man like this teacher do to resolve his predicament? It may not be pleasant to read or reflect on, but the reality is that most people in his situation are not going to resolve their inner conflicts by themselves. They will do the best they can—try to do nothing therapeutically and minimize their problems, limping along with their inner burdens and hopefully avoiding major catastrophes. They may use friends or relatives to unload their troubles, getting no real help but only temporary relief. They may go back to the family case worker or the minister—and there are a great many people who continue to use whatever help is available, even though they and the helpers know that more is needed.

This teacher went one step further, and returned to the analyst to discuss other possibilities. Would it be possible to see the analyst only once, or at most twice, a week? Could he accomplish something in a few months or a year? And, finally, was there any possibility of lowering the hourly fee?

These questions have been on the minds of a great number of people who know that analysis is necessary for them, but who cannot afford it. In trying to answer them, it would be well to begin with the last one, asked often and with good reason by many people: Why is analysis so expensive?

The expense of a full analysis is partly due to the hourly fee, but more significantly to the fact that the process of re-living requires hundreds of hours, which should be spaced as close together as possible for maximum effectiveness. In the opening chapter, I suggested eight hundred to a thousand hours as one possible measure for the length of a full analysis, and explained the necessity of having the weekly sessions as close together as possible. Even if the analyst took an extremely low hourly fee of five dollars—which would be less than the hourly fee of a qualified tutor in a college—the analysis would run to five thousand dollars, a sum that would be out of the range of the average American income, even if it were divided over a five-year period. And just the fact that analysis requires a consecutive amount of time explains why it cannot be a popular method of treatment.

This is, of course, one important reason why psychoanalysis, as a preferred treatment method, has not found the place in our society that its scientific validity deserves. It also explains, in part, why only a small segment of the population has had any direct, first-hand experience with trained analysts. It explains further why there is a continuous search for short-cut methods, for therapies that do not require so much of the patient's time and money. In this chapter, I shall discuss some of these attempts—the applications and derivatives of analysis found in clinics and in private practice.

The average hourly fee of a full psychoanalysis, ranging from about fifteen to thirty dollars, reflects, of course, inflationary trends, as do many fees for hourly services in the professions and trades. Less than ten years ago, hourly analytic fees ranged from ten to twenty dollars, which today approximates the fees of qualified clinics. If one were to arrive at the basis of the hourly fee, one could proceed in a number of ways—take the financial equivalent of pre-analytic and analytic training, plus the therapist's personal analysis, and compare it to the initial financial investment required in other professions and trades. This would not be a very scientific method, but there is no accurate way of establishing the basis of fees for professional services. No matter what the pre-analytic training of the analyst—medicine, psychology, social work, or other fields—in order to qualify, a man must have had four years of college and from three to six years of graduate training, with one to two years of interneships in any of the fields. This means that the prospective analyst has to finance from seven to nine years of studies, after high school. To this must be added from three to five years of analytic training, making a total of twelve to fourteen years of study. If one took two thousand dollars as a low average for a college or graduate-school year, the analyst would have to spend some twenty-five thousand dollars prior to practicing analysis. To this we must add the cost of the prospective analyst's required personal analysis— say, fifteen thousand dollars, a minimum figure—bringing the total to some forty thousand dollars of investment, prior to practice. While many practitioners are able to charge fees while still in training, the total cost of their training would still come to approximately this amount, which may be considered conservative and is probably more often closer to fifty thousand dollars. This initial investment is considerably higher than the training investment in other professions, and while the analyst's hourly fees are high for the average American, the return to the practitioner of his training investment is possibly lower than that of people in related professions.

Since many analysts come from the field of medicine, it may be appropriate to compare their rates with the hourly fees of a general practitioner. It is probably fair to assume that a very reasonable office visit to a neighborhood family physician costs five dollars. Some practitioners may charge as much as ten dollars per visit. From estimates made by a number of general practitioners, an office visit may average fifteen to twenty minutes, which, at a very low rate of five dollars per visit, gives the practitioner between fifteen and twenty dollars per hour. This compares fairly to the average of the analyst, whose initial training investment is higher.

But even with the relatively high hourly fees, analysis would not be outside the economic range of most people if the treatment method did not require several hundred times the hourly fee. The first thought that comes to mind, then, is to shorten the length of treatment. The consequence of such attempts is, of course, that the results are not the same as with a full analysis. Since a full analysis is not a luxury, cutting down on the length is not like cutting out fancy trimmings in a house, but more like building a less solid structure. Without carrying the analogy too far, it may be suggested that the aim of a full analysis is to make the core of the personality so solid that it will last, hopefully, a lifetime. As in any solid structure, you can't give up certain vital parts without doing injustice to the job as a whole.

The American tendency to mass-produce, to streamline goods, books, and life, has also affected treatment methods. While daily sessions, at least five times a week, were customary in Europe, and still are in some European countries, American analysts have settled for four weekly sessions as more or less standard. There are also analysts who see their patients even less frequently. The question is whether this quantitative reduction of work does not seriously affect the quality, and most analysts would agree that twice-a-week treatment cannot be considered a full analysis. These analysts may themselves have some patients whom they see twice a week, but they are not attempting a full analysis with them; instead, they have deliberately limited treatment goals and treatment methods. This kind of analytic therapy, which may be compared to the work with adolescents described in a previous chapter, is often necessary for either economic or clinical reasons. And since the earning potential of patients often increases during treatment, it is sometimes possible to shift from a modified form of therapy to full analysis. In cases where normal aggression is directed inward, toward some form of self-destruction, instead of outward, toward realistic goals, patients have found that during therapy they have become more effective in their work and, instead of feeling beaten by life, have spoken up and made realistic and appropriate demands, so that their incomes have increased.

A few illustrations may clarify this: A young woman working as a secretary had been underpaid for years, according to the going wages for her category of work. She felt, when she began therapy, that this was all she "deserved" and that she was lucky to be paid at all. Curiously enough, she had been given increasing responsibility in her jobs, becoming, after a very short time, an important part of every office in which she had worked. But her salary was not raised, because she needed to give her employers the impression that she did not care about money and was working for the fun of it. Although she lived with her parents, the family was far from well off financially and even the two times a week that she visited the analyst put a strain on her resources. Besides, it would have meant a great deal to her to be paid well for her work. A massive wall of unconscious guilt prevented her from accepting her realistic goals. She had to deny her wishes to be successful and financially remunerated for her labors.

As she began to work through some of her guilt and her unrealistic attitudes toward money, she found it less humiliating to be paid. She saw that she was as good as or better than other workers in her office and was able to take a stand for herself. After one year of therapy, she had increased her income sufficiently to come three times a week. The analyst lowered his fee, and after a few months took her on for a fourth session, agreeing to carry the balance until after her analysis was completed.

To take another example, a young man in the advertising field, with considerable artistic talent, knew that his future in his firm was limited, but found it impossible to consider a change of jobs. His relationship to the senior partner was like that of a son to a stern father. When the older man spoke, the patient listened and did what he was told. He had been employed in the firm for many years, and suffered from the phobia that if he were fired, he would never again get another employer like the one he now had. Although many of his colleagues did free-lance work in addition to their regular jobs, and were in no way barred by their firms from earning this additional income, the patient considered this disloyal to the boss. His friends tried to convince him of his talent, his ability to free-lance, to try part-time work, at least, but the patient could not see himself in such a role. Not to be able to count on his weekly pay check—no matter how small—was to him equivalent to being destitute, and to work for other people in his spare time seemed dishonest.

Although his employer himself made it clear that the young man did not owe any loyalty to the firm beyond the time that he was paid for, the patient did not believe this, and took it as another sign of generosity from his boss. He felt that he would betray a trust if he were to take the old man up on his own words. It seemed to him that success, and particularly financial success, was immoral and dangerous. He had a strong need to remain poor and in straitened circumstances.

While it was not possible to work through to the deepest roots of his illness—which had many other complicated symptoms —the patient did succeed, in two years of twice-weekly therapy, in throwing off his fear of earning money. He was about ready to begin a full analysis when he was offered an excellent job opportunity abroad, and he started analysis there, since he was now able to afford it.

These two examples are not offered as a solution to the economic problem psychoanalysis poses. It would be unrealistic to attempt to propose any solution at this time, since the economic aspect is closely tied in with the social and cultural aspects. The fact that there are relatively few psychoanalysts is itself a significant factor in considering the problem from a social point of view. Even if the cost could be reduced so drastically that anybody could afford psychoanalysis, who would give the treatment? Even if all the differences could be resolved and all agreements on background could be settled, even if all universities undertook the training of analysts on such a basis, it has been estimated that the gap between supply and demand would not even begin to be filled for twenty-five years. And there is no basis for assuming that these theoretical differences about training in all the psychotherapies will be resolved in the near future.

There are partial answers. Some insurance companies have recognized psychoanalysis or other forms of psychotherapy as valid claims, which brings this treatment method within the reach of some middle-class incomes. One of the most widespread partial answers is the low- or medium-priced clinic. The fees in such clinics average ten dollars per therapeutic session. There are also psychoanalytic training schools that offer full analytic treatment for a fraction of this amount.

The analysis in these analytic training institutes is carried on by analysts in training, as described in the chapter on training. Since these analysts are themselves very carefully supervised, sometimes by several supervisors, and at the same time are observed in their class work and seminars, their lack of experience is amply compensated for by the control of the psychoanalytic institute. I recently referred a young student of chemistry, who was working for his degree and earned about four thousand dollars a year as a part-time instructor, to the oldest and best-established of the psychoanalytic institutes. After submitting a very thorough autobiography, and being interviewed by three different officers of the institute, he was accepted for a full—five-times-a-week—analysis. The hourly cost was computed on the basis of his income and expenses, and was set at five and a half dollars.

There is no limit placed on the length of his analysis, and he can be certain of a complete analysis—whether it takes four or more years—at a cost he can afford. Unhappily, there are only very few analysts in training at any one time, and it is easy to imagine how many applications for this service accumulate over the years. The institutes base their selection of patients on many criteria, the needs of the patient and of the training analysts, the areas of particular research going on at a given time, prognosis, and expected difficulties in treatment.

These services offered by training institutes of psychoanalysis are the only ones that provide full analytic treatment for a minimum fee. With the great demand for full analytic services and the infinitesimally small supply, an applicant like the young scientist is in about the same position as a scholar who has won an exceptional fellowship, or a very extensive government-sponsored grant.

It is remarkable how many of these educational fellowships are open to gifted and promising people today, while, to the best of my knowledge, no foundation so far has seen fit to make the same opportunity available for work in mental health. Judging by the increased efficiency of some of our most talented people after they have had a thorough analysis, it would seem to make sense to suggest that fellowships or government grants be made available to talented students, just as educational opportunities are offered to them. The late Ernest Kris, in fact, conducted a special analytic research project at Yale University for particularly gifted scientists and artists, most of whom could never have been in analysis without some special private contributions. Perhaps in the future there will be a foundation that will offer a full analysis to people who meet certain educational and clinical criteria. This would be a selective use of psychoanalysis, having the same aim as educational grants—encouraging people who seem most likely to make outstanding contributions to society. But even if such a foundation were to be created, it would not answer the larger question of therapy for the majority who need it, who are not exceptionally gifted but who want to be healthy just the same.

What actually is available at lower fees at this time?

There are a great many services in the mental-hygiene field, and they have all been influenced by psychoanalysis to some degree. However, they are not psychoanalytic therapy or psychoanalysis. The mental-hygiene services in this country embrace the many medical groups that are springing up in various regions, which include psychiatrists as well as other specialists; mental-hygiene clinics in many hospitals; the child-guidance clinics attached to many school systems; travelling mental-hygiene units, covering part of a county; social agencies; family-case-work services; and the guidance and counselling facilities in many communities, including reading clinics and pastoral counselling.

In the context of this book, though, it would be misleading to confuse the general mental-hygiene services with specific psychoanalytic ones. Both are vitally necessary areas of therapy, but they are not the same and should not be confused. However, in addition to the psychoanalytic clinics in training institutes, there are also clinics—mainly private—in some metropolitan centers, which are pertinent to the subject of this book. These clinics do not offer the same full psychoanalytic services as the training institutes, but they do offer psychotherapy based on psychoanalytic principles. In other words, these private clinics offer at a much lower cost services similar to some private analysts who see patients two or three times a week.

To avoid confusion, it may be helpful to emphasize that I am not referring here to "another form of therapy" but am still discussing psychoanalysis. Many psychoanalysts, as I mentioned before, conduct, besides full and complete analysis, less intensive and modified forms of analytic psychotherapy, similar to the treatment described with children and young people. It is an exception, however, rather than the rule in the practice of psychoanalysts. Therefore, only a very small number of patients can be seen by private analysts on the modified, two- or three-times-a-week basis. Therefore, medium-priced clinics—with fees ranging between eight and fourteen dollars an hour—fill an important community need.

What are such clinics like? How are they operated? Who are the therapists, who are the patients? What actually goes on? To get an inside view, let us go back to the teacher who discovered that he needed therapy and could not afford a full analysis. Let us assume that the analyst whom he saw once or twice referred him to one of the private clinics in his community. Since these clinics customarily service a given area in a large community, they are often named after the community. Let us call the clinic, for our discussion, the Maple View Center for Psychotherapy.

Mr. Jones, the teacher, found the clinic located on the main floor of an apartment house in a residential neighborhood. Mrs. Walker, the psychiatric social worker who greeted him, may herself have had an analysis. In any case, she had had four years of college and at least two more years in a graduate school for social work. Some of her classes included psychoanalytic theory, as applied to the specialized field of psychiatric social work. She may have worked previously in social agencies, or family case work, or perhaps in mental-hygiene clinics in hospitals. She was particularly skilled at the art of interviewing, which requires specialized training and supervised-field-work experience. She is a vital part of any clinic team, whether it is in a psychoanalytically oriented clinic like Maple View, or a child-guidance clinic attached to a public-school system.

Before seeing Mr. Jones, Mrs. Walker had read the receptionist's write-up of the referral and may have phoned the analyst to discuss the case in more detail. She would have a first diagnostic impression of the patient, and would correct this as she met him face to face. The purpose of the interview is to form a more meaningful clinical picture of the patient, based on as many solid facts as possible, together with a thorough description of the social and economic issues involved. The social worker would have to recognize where the painful areas of the patient's personality were located, and make distinctions between information he gave her that was valid, and other information that might not represent objective facts. Her job is not to treat the patient but to get as much understanding of him as possible, since her written report of the interview forms the basis of the "intake conference" held after other specialists have seen the patient.

This report may contain some topical headings to give an over-all view of some of the subjects covered; it may start with a section called Presenting Problems, and be followed by Clinical History, Family Background, Social and Economic Problems, Work History, Early Childhood, Tentative Diagnostic Impressions, Summary, and Recommendations.

In the interview, which would not have been conducted along these organized lines, but would range all over, Mrs. Walker would explain the intake, the fee, and the clinical procedure to Mr. Jones. She might also ask him to fill out a financial statement, which would form the basis for the fee to be set by the intake committee. Mr. Jones would learn that he would be seen by a psychiatrist, and possibly also a psychologist, for some psychological tests, after which the three workers would meet and then let him know about his first therapeutic appointment with his regular therapist. During this meeting, the number of hours per week and the fee would also be decided, based on information supplied by Mr. Jones.

In some clinics, giving a battery of psychological tests is routine; in others it is reserved for special situations only. The testing is done by a clinical psychologist. He may be a regular member of the clinic, also qualified to treat patients, or he may have limited his training to testing. He is like the X-ray specialist, who does not treat patients medically, but has developed special skills for interpreting clinical findings.

The psychologist has had his regular college degree, plus five years of graduate training, including internship in a mental hospital, and possibly he has also earned his doctorate in psychology. He sees the patient for one or two sessions, in which he administers a series of standardized psychological tests, possibly including the Rorschach (or ink-blot) test. The patient's answers or associations are noted by the psychologist on specialized forms. On seeing the patient for the second time, the psychologist—whom we shall call Dr. Greeley—will probably give him a number of other tests as well.

Some of these will be so-called projective tests. One of the better-known ones would be the Thematic Apperception Test, usually called the T.A.T. In this and similar tests, the patient is asked to project himself into imaginary situations and react as if he were involved in them. Toward this purpose, he is shown a series of standardized pictures depicting various situations. He will be asked to make up some story suggested to him by the drawing. As in the Rorschach test, the answer possibilities are unlimited, but here, too, certain characteristic responses will be suggestive of certain personality traits.

Dr. Greeley may also give some standardized intelligence tests, measuring various levels of perception, observation, reasoning ability—any number of inquiries into the human mind. There are a great number of other tests that will be chosen by the psychologist, according to the needs of the patient.

When the testing sessions are over, Dr. Greeley will get to work interpreting the various results. Here is where his special talents and skills come in. He will interpret each of the separate tests and tabulate them according to standardized procedures. Gradually, he will form a first diagnostic impression of the patient's personality, which he will want to check further by comparing the tabulated results of the various tests. If some responses are very puzzling to him, he may look into the specialized literature, and will perhaps want to consult with experienced colleagues on some aspects of his findings. When he is certain that he can back up all of his impressions with scientifically acceptable findings, he will write up each of the test results and then come up with a final psychological report, which he will turn over to the clinic committee, which already has Mrs. Walker's report.

After this, Mr. Jones will return for his final evaluation interview with Dr. Robbins, the clinic's psychiatrist—a physician with an M.D. degree who has specialized in psychiatry, after interne and residence experience in mental hospitals. He will have read Mrs. Walker's and Dr. Greeley's reports and will keep these facts in mind as he conducts his interview. One of the first facts he will ascertain is whether the patient is psychotic or not. After years of working with psychotics, he will be particularly qualified to establish this vital fact very quickly. He will be able to spot insanity or its potential instantly; he will recognize whether the patient's contact with reality is so tenuous that he can go off into insanity very easily. He will consider the potential of suicide, dangerous violence, socially unacceptable perversions. Once he has established that Mr. Jones is not psychotic, but suffers from a form of neurosis, he will be able to describe the neurosis in clinical terms and make recommendations for therapy.

In his interview, he will pay attention to the kind of material the patient brings to him, his way of relating to the doctor, the degree of bizarre or inappropriate responses, the attempt to cover up dangerous personality aspects with a forced kind of rationality. He may use information that was given to Mrs. Walker and go into detail about some aspects that seem clinically significant to him. If the patient should come up with physical symptoms, he would be interested in them and possibly refer Mr. Jones to one of the clinic's panel physicians for a checkup.

After his interview, Dr. Robbins too will write up his findings and send them to the clinic committee. While Mr. Jones is waiting for his first regular therapeutic appointment, the clinic committee will meet to discuss all three reports. This committee consists of Mrs. Walker, Dr. Greeley, Dr. Robbins, and the administrative or clinical director of the clinic. In the conference, the three reports are read and discussed by all the committee members. There may be discrepancies in the findings of each of the specialists that will have to be resolved by a thorough clinical discussion. Since each of the three workers has written his report in considerable detail, it is possible to compare the findings and arrive at a clinical diagnosis.

One of the points to be settled in this conference is the fee. The social and economic facts are considered together with the psychological and psychiatric findings. Depending on the final diagnosis, it will be possible to decide how many times the patient should be seen to get satisfactory results, which in turn affects the hourly fee. Another item that has to be decided upon is the choice of therapist for this particular patient. There may be ten or fifteen therapists on the staff of the clinic, full-time or part-time. They may have had a full analysis or have had other psychotherapeutic experiences. They come from different academic backgrounds; some have more, some less experience. In addition to these factual differences, there are the significant but not easily ascertainable differences in their personalities. Each therapist has his own style of working; each is more or less gifted for one patient or another.

There is also the practical question of how many patients these therapists are presently seeing, and whether their days in the clinic—if they work part-time—will coincide with the days and hours suitable for the patient. Each of the therapists has a supervisor, and the intake committee may defer the decision on the choice of therapist until they have conferred with the supervisor of one of the therapists under consideration. Most likely, the clinic conducts some in-service training seminars in a variety of clinical topics. One of the members of the intake committee may teach one or more of these seminars, and know some of the therapists from previous case discussion.

Eventually, all the findings will be summarized, a letter will be sent to Mr. Jones in which he is told the name of his therapist, his appointment hours are stated, and he is invited to begin treatment at the Maple View Clinic.

The procedure described up to this point is patterned after the traditional child-guidance clinic, in which a three-part team always works together in a similar way. The approach is so typical of child-guidance work that special treatment approaches have evolved, leading to the formation of one of the largest psychiatric organizations, in which the three-part team is fairly represented.

This organization is called the American Orthopsychiatric Association. (Orthopsychiatry has been defined as "the study of both normal and deviant behavior by the combined efforts of the behavioral sciences. These include psychiatry, psychology, social work, psychoanalysis, medicine, nursing, sociology, education, and anthropology. While this interdisciplinary approach was first applied to children, it has also proven helpful in work with adults and families.") As this definition suggests, workers in community clinics—whether for adults or children, or both—may or may not have had a full psychoanalysis or practice a modified form of psychoanalysis. Many clinics accept therapists who practice other forms of therapy, and other clinics specialize in a particular form of therapy. Clinics affiliated with training institutes, such as those founded by Karen Horney and Harry Stack Sullivan, Carl Jung and Alfred Adler, prefer to employ therapists trained in their specific methods of therapy.

For the purpose of discussing medium- or low-priced clinics in the context of this book, we have chosen the Maple View Clinic with the assumption that its therapists' approach is psychoanalytic. The therapist who will see Mr. Jones will conduct a form of psychotherapy that is psychoanalytically oriented. Before he begins, he will have his recommendations from the intake committee, suggesting therapeutic approaches, prognosis, and the amount of the fee. All the recommendations from the committee will be in the nature of suggestions. The therapist, together with the patient, will arrive at definite decisions. They will talk about the suggested fee in the first hour, and will consider how many times a week the patient can conveniently be seen.

In no case will the therapist in the clinic conduct a full analysis. He himself may not as yet have finished his own analysis and be in the middle of his analytic training experience. In most cases, he is a younger man with considerable financial responsibilities and probably with a growing family. From the average clinic fee of ten dollars, he may receive five or seven dollars per hour, while the remaining amount covers the clinic overhead. He is probably able to give two, or at most three, days to the clinic, and is expected to carry as many patients as possible in order to meet the community's great demand. As was suggested earlier, the character of his analytic therapy in some ways resembles that described in the chapter on therapy with young people.

In terms of therapeutic gains, let us speculate about the possible results in the case of Mr. Jones, the schoolteacher. If the roots of his illness go very deep—and this the tests and the intake interviews would show—it is likely that his problems would not be sufficiently resolved in the Maple View Clinic to assure him of a sound marital relationship. While this kind of prediction is difficult enough to make about anyone, it is certainly not possible to be definite about it with a severely neurotic patient. On the other hand, it is quite possible that the analytic therapy in the clinic would protect him sufficiently to prevent recurrences of that frightening episode in the classroom that made him seek help in the first place. It is probably fair to say that clinics can achieve symptomatic changes, help the patient and the community through greater inner protection against uncontrolled, instinctual acting out, and help people to lead more satisfying and fruitful lives.

ELEVEN

·

The Ending of Analysis

We started this book by asking, "What is analysis?" We are concluding it by asking, "When is it finished?"

There are as many questions about the end of analysis as there are about the beginning and the middle. For example, how do you know when it is finished, and who decides this, anyway? Is there a definite date on which you leave the analyst's office for good?

One thing is certain: analyses do end. Some people have the notion that once you start an analysis, it goes on practically forever, in one form or another. Some people have to get injections from their physicians most of their life, and there are forms of psychotherapy in which a patient continues to receive some psychological support indefinitely, but psychoanalysis is a form of therapy that comes to a very clear and defined end.

This does not mean that the patient has worked out every last inner conflict, or that he now is "one hundred per cent healthy." Many people go as far as they and their analysts feel they are ready to go, and then decide to stop. Have they completed their analysis, and is it necessary to continue even when one no longer feels interested? This raises the core question: What does completion of an analysis really mean?

Usually we talk about completing something when we have done the job we started out to do. What did we start out to do in analysis? We said in the first chapter that psychoanalysis is a treatment method particularly for disturbances of the sense of self-preservation. We spelled out what we meant by that. It would follow that the job is done when the sense of self-preservation is no longer disturbed, when the patient is functioning in such a way that his self-interest is usually maintained. How can one tell whether this is the case or not? Perhaps we might look at a summary of an analysis before we consider some criteria that could determine with fair accuracy to what degree self-interest is maintained.

A young and attractive woman in her early thirties, from a comfortable, conventional background, went into analysis when she finally recognized that her sexual behavior was so self-destructive that it had nearly wrecked her brilliant career as a research biologist. For years she had been involved with men who not only openly exploited her financially but mistreated her physically. Not only would she support her lovers and turn her apartment over to them, she would also perform the most menial tasks, getting sexual satisfaction out of being ordered around and humiliated. One of her lovers demanded that she procure other women for him, and made her look on while he made love to them. Another lover demanded absolute cleanliness in her apartment and, after a white-glove inspection, would punish her for any dust he found on the furniture. The punishment would be the over-the-knee kind of spanking given to humiliate children. All of these activities gave her the greatest sexual satisfaction, and while she hated herself for playing these games, she found them too exciting to give up.

Another lover made her stand in a corner, partially undressed and waiting to be punished for losing valuables, such as a watch, rings, or money. The losing of things of value, together with the giving away of precious possessions, was another symptom of long standing, even before it was connected with her sexual perversions.

At the same time she was very successful in her university, where she was engaged in research involving drugs. When one of her lovers insisted that she turn over to him for commercial use a formula from her laboratory that was being tried out and was not for public consumption, she became desperate and asked the head of her department for help. It was then that she was referred to an analyst and began therapy.

In her long and complicated analysis, some of the symptoms disappeared after a relatively short time. She stopped losing valuables and giving away her treasured possessions. Her breathing difficulties—which had no organic basis—vanished; so did her affairs with married men. By the second year of analysis, she had stopped seeing men altogether and was free of overt symptoms. But this, of course, had not been the purpose of the analysis. The basic conflicts that had been acted out in her sexual behavior needed to be fully analyzed and worked through before she could arrive at a true inner balance.

By the process of free association and analysis of dreams, the component parts of her neurosis gradually became visible. To put it in the briefest possible form, she had solved her disappointment over being a female by denying her feminine role and concentrating all her energies upon intellectual pursuits that to her were neither male nor female but "pure brain," as she put it. She was of foreign birth and had a first name that could be either masculine or feminine. She was happiest when she received her doctorate, so that no sexual identification was necessary when she was addressed. There had been a period in her late adolescence when she nearly got involved in homosexual relationships, but she could not accept this role either, wanting to be neither male nor female.

The reasons for her strong rejection of the feminine role—which took place when she was about five—did not emerge until late in her analysis, and involved a detailed understanding of her very early life and her relationships to her parents and siblings. Her rejection of herself as a girl had not been conscious, and there were no overt difficulties until the first potential homosexual relationships threatened during her second year of high school. Although she dressed prettily, was flirtatious, went to dances, and had dates, she gradually became aware of a growing self-hate, particularly as she got prettier and received more and more compliments. It started slowly. A boy would tell her that she had beautiful blond curls, and she would find herself looking into the mirror and cutting off the very curls that had been praised. Shortly after her legs were admired, she had two consecutive accidents that necessitated their being bandaged. This self-hate extended to other behavior. She would be so rude that the boy she was with would turn nasty, and this was one of her "pleasures." Gradually she sought out boys and men who abused her, while she continued to shine in college and academic work. Eventually this led to the sexual behavior that finally brought her to analysis.

When was her analysis finished? Not until she had analyzed most of the deeper causes of her infantile conflict over being a girl could she begin to accept herself as a woman, and expect the same respect, as a woman, that she received as a scientist. Only when she could like herself as a woman—when she no longer needed to fight reality—could she consider sexuality as connected with love, rather than hate. Not until she had fully resolved her very early conflict, and had, incidentally, given up the fantasy that she could be either sex or neither—and thereby better than other mortals—could she realize what her self-interest was.

Until this conflict had been analyzed, part of her mental energy was used for self-destruction, rather than self-preservation. When she found herself saying in her analysis that she had resented being introduced as a scientist at a party, she was at first surprised to find that what she wanted most was to be accepted as a woman, not as a "brain." Very gradually she found that she chose new and quite different people as friends, people who did not use her or exploit her, but cared about her and were kind to her. The first time a man sent her flowers after a lecture, she cried with happiness. What had moved her most were the words on the card: "The paper was very interesting, but the flowers are for a lovely woman." At this point she was clearly nearing the end of her analysis.

Just as we enumerated in the opening chapter some criteria that suggested the need for analysis, it is possible to list corresponding ones that suggest the analysis is complete. One would be the ability to do something seriously, rather than play at it. This means that a patient is able to carry through and complete work with some degree of pleasure, instead of an irrational sense of duty. It may include the removal of psychological or physical symptoms that originally prevented the person from working at something seriously—e.g., in a man who makes his living by reading, headaches, or blurred vision, without any organic basis; repeated attacks of dizziness or near-fainting spells in an actor, prior to openings.

Another indicator of the end of an analysis may be a person's ability to discharge aggression in a socially acceptable way. This means that the patient has stopped hating himself or blowing up in sudden rages against somebody else; that he is able to say no without guilt, to disagree without becoming either defensive or petulant. It might mean that he could have empathy with others —that is, feel deeply with them, without losing his sense of identity or his values.

Increased social contacts and interests would mean that a patient had been able to form meaningful relationships without being desperately dependent on them. Still another sign of a person's sense of self-preservation is his capacity to enjoy the other sex, which may or may not include his ability to form meaningful sexual relationships. It could simply mean the ability to share interests with the other sex without feelings of self-consciousness or competition. In any case, it means relationships in which one's sense of self-preservation is maintained, and one has neither to get hurt nor to hurt somebody else, knowingly or unknowingly.

Another indication of a patient's readiness to end analysis is the way his love manifests itself. When a person is ready to form permanent love relationships, his choice of a partner is relatively free, and he can become deeply attached without becoming dependent in an infantile way or surrounding his partner with fantasies or relying on the judgments of the outside world. The way love manifests itself may be indicated by the ability to accept a partner or another love object, such as a member of one's family, without necessarily agreeing with or approving of everything they do; or by the readiness to stand by and accept a loved person's success or failure without a sense of self-glorification or burdening pity.

Perhaps the most inclusive sign that analysis has served its purpose is the patient's emotional balance—his ability to steer a steady course through his daily chores, to react appropriately to people and situations, to absorb new and foreign thoughts or actions with a sense of reflection, and to suspend judgment until the most mature parts of his personality can operate; his readiness to accept his mistakes and acknowledge himself wrong with-

out guilt or self-mockery, to give up the status quo when this is
called for by his self-interest; his awareness of the objective limitations in his environment and the inner boundaries of his own
personality and body, by appropriate reactions to illness, accidents,
tragedies. There may be the ability to recover from severe shocks
and a continued sense of self-preservation in all situations.

As in the suggested criteria in Chapter I for determining
someone's need for analysis, no one of the criteria for termination is by itself too meaningful. It is, rather, the combination of
many of these that suggests a patient's readiness to plan the end
of his analysis. And all of the criteria involve clinical judgments on the part of the analyst and judgment values on the
part of the patient.

It cannot be emphasized too strongly that there can be no
absolutes in such criteria, and that many of them may strike one
reader or another as idealizations of normality. These readers will
appreciate Freud's paper "Analysis Terminable and Intermina-
ble," written in 1937, in which he cautioned against exaggeration
by saying, "It cannot be disputed that analysts do not in their
own personalities wholly come up to their standards of psychic
normality which they set for their patients." As for his own tests
for termination of analysis, he made the general suggestion that
"when the best psychological conditions for the functioning of the
ego have been established, analysis has accomplished its task."

This is a clinical statement, involving an understanding of
the functioning of the ego. One way in which such evaluation
can be made more objective is through psychological tests, given
by a clinical psychologist who knows nothing about the patient.
Some analysts use before-and-after psychological testing, like the
use of X rays before and after surgery. These tests are additional
verifications of basic personality changes in a patient.

However, such testing procedures can be only complementary to the clinical understanding of the analyst. As with every other phase of psychoanalysis, the patient's associations are the most reliable indicators of the way his ego is functioning. The experienced analyst knows the indicators that signal the coming of the final analytic phase. Frequently the patient notices a lessening of interest in his regular analytic sessions, quite different from the strong positive or negative feelings he had about them in the early phase of his analysis. More and more often, his associations have to do with experiences involving parting, perhaps memories of the past, when leaving parents was difficult or even caused anxiety. There will be changes in the contents of his dreams, and his associations to them will sometimes suggest that the dream was so close to reality that it could almost have happened. The patient will think of other, more important things on which to spend his money, and will resent the expense of his analysis in a very different way than he did during the other phases of analysis, when he hated the analyst. Frequently he will talk about stopping analysis in the near future, and often analyst and patient plan a termination date, perhaps four or six months ahead.

Once such a date has been agreed upon, patients frequently begin to wonder whether they have made a mistake, and ask for reassurance from the analyst. This kind of anxiety is as much part of the analysis as all its other aspects, and will be worked through with free associations, as before. Just as the patient begins and ends his analysis by associating freely, the analyst continues to try to perceive the complex interplay of the various parts of the patient's mental anatomy. He relates these to his original diagnosis and prognosis of the case, so that he can make a responsible judgment of his patient's readiness to continue analysis or to recognize that he has gone as far as he is able to at this point in his life. It is part of the skilled analyst's job to distinguish between a pa-

tient's hesitation to work through some particularly difficult problem and his readiness to discontinue analysis.

While some patients show eagerness to end the analytic work
before they have gone as far as they could, others develop something like an addiction to analysis and cannot imagine an end to
the process. There seems to be general agreement that the con-
clusion of an analysis by mutual consent has the best prognosis.
Most analysts continue with the regular sessions, instead of taper-
ing off to fewer sessions per week, as is frequently the case in
other forms of psychotherapy.

Once an analysis has ended successfully, many patients have
no difficulty leaving the analyst, and do not experience any desire
whatsoever to return for more sessions or for brief consultations.
For them, the treatment is finished and they have no need to
think or talk much about their completed analysis.

There are other patients who *do* wish to return for occasional
sessions after the analysis is over. This procedure is usually not
encouraged because such visits cannot be used for further exploratory analysis, but only for a general kind of reassurance. There is
nothing wrong with this service or with occasional social contacts
with the analyst after an analysis is completed, except that it
makes it impossible for the patient ever to use the analyst again
for real analytic work, should this become necessary in later life.
As a rule, people do not need to return for a second analysis, but
such occasions have arisen, owing to unusual life circumstances.
Other friendly people may be used for reassurance, and a great
many people are available for social contact. It seems practical to
keep the analyst in his analytic role and not attempt to make
other uses of this relationship.

This does not mean that patients do not sometimes come
back to see their analyst for an occasional consultation, years after
their analysis was completed. But when patients find reasons to

wish to return to the familiar office shortly after the analysis has ended, it is likely that they are having difficulty giving up an experience that has been deeply helpful to them. One patient telephoned shortly after the last session to refer a good friend, almost as though she were saying, "Since I have no legitimate reason to continue, I can at least send a good friend to you instead." It is similar to the pleasure we all get when we introduce a friend to a good experience we have had. At times these good intentions may be a little misplaced, particularly when the friend who is urged to consider psychoanalysis will have no part of it. Perhaps one of the most difficult lessons for a helpful person to learn is the rule that one cannot, under any circumstances, talk somebody else into accepting psychoanalysis, or, for that matter, any kind of psychotherapy. Selling is a highly developed skill in this country, but even in this day and age, with all the techniques of persuasion known to men and Madison Avenue, you cannot sell anybody the desire to get well. If the secondary gain in the illness is stronger than the wish to get rid of the neurosis, selling or persuasion, tricks or promises, will not do it.

What makes this hard to accept is the fact that you or I can plainly see what is the matter with a friend, but this friend may not feel the same way, and will not appreciate our mixing in his business. A case in point is the young scientist mentioned earlier in this chapter. Through the years, she would cry bitter tears over her miserable relationships with men. She would implore friends and relatives to help her, and many of them advised one form of therapy or another, depending on their own experiences or orientation. She took down all the names and considered making calls. On a few occasions, she even made appointments to see a therapist. Once she actually did go, on the insistent urging of one of her friends. She had a long interview, liked the therapist, inquired into all the details—and did not return for therapy. The sick gratifications of her sexual behavior outweighed her decision to "do something about it" every time, until the balance was tipped and there was enough pain to motivate her into starting analysis. As long as she was able to keep her professional life—and the many satisfactions it provided—separate from the symptoms of her illness, she avoided facing her inner conflicts. Once the results of her disturbed sexual behavior were about to ruin her professional life, she faced the issue and started to give up her neurotic satisfactions. What, one could speculate, would have happened if the constructive and the destructive parts of her personality had not come so dangerously close to each other? Would she have continued to live in constant, never resolved conflicts?

There is certainly ample evidence all around us of people with deep inner conflicts who are struggling to maintain an inner balance without getting any effective help. It is commonly stated that "one in ten people is mentally ill or psychologically disturbed," as reported in the most recent authoritative report to Congress by the Joint Commission on Mental Illness and Health. This is a staggering and frightening figure. Yet even this does not tell the story of the additional millions who do not become sick enough to require hospitalization, but who are not well enough to live satisfying lives. The final test for our way of life will be the mental and physical health of the population, rather than the so-called standard of living, which includes everything but a sound inner balance.

What contribution has psychoanalysis made toward the mental health of the population? We said in the first chapter that it is a treatment method, not a philosophy. It cannot eliminate poverty or prevent wars. Does this mean that psychoanalysis has not made significant contributions toward the mental health of the population?

Two of the great explorers of our time once put their minds

to such basic questions as the prevention of war—Freud, the explorer of the soul, and Einstein, the explorer of the cosmos. In an exchange of letters, Einstein posed the question, "Why war?" and asked Freud to reply. Freud did reply. The time was 1932, the place Vienna. Barely four months after the ink had dried on the letters, the Nazis burned the Reichstag in Berlin, providing the fireworks for Hitler's rise to power and the beginning of the Second World War.

The Einstein-Freud correspondence, undertaken under the auspices of the League of Nations, was first published in Paris in 1933, not long before the two scientists had to abandon their offices and libraries and flee the pursuing hordes. What did they say in this untimely discussion? Freud undertook to answer the question because he saw it as a theoretical discussion between "a physicist and a psychologist," not as an attempt "to make practical proposals." In these published letters, he talks about the origins of violence in man, the relation between love and hate, and ends by saying that "whatever fosters the growth of culture works at the same time against war."

Usually we think of culture as an advance in human relations, as a result of the forces of civilization. We think of it as an enlightening, progressive force away from the primitive, uncivilized forces in the individual and society. Perhaps the most significant factor in comprehending human nature is the discovery of the unconscious—a part of the mind that is timeless and unknown. The discovery of the fact that the same primitive and uncivilized instincts that have characterized the most primitive cultures and the most inhuman behavior continue to exist in our unconscious mind—that barbarism continues to exist potentially in all of us, regardless of the particular social organization at any one time or place in history—has been of the most far-reaching significance in the development of human understanding and, with it, of human civilization.

We have always known that there is a residue of primitive instincts and primitive hostilities in the individual and in many societies. Until Freud, we were not able to pierce the secrets of this dark, unknown part of the mind. The breaking of barriers, the opening up of new terrain, is always significant for civilization. We have been astounded by the breaking of sound barriers, the piercing of the ocean bottom, the flight around the earth. Can there be a more significant discovery than the hitherto unknown part of the human mind—the light into the unconscious that determines the greater part of all our thoughts, feelings, and, finally, actions?

During our lifetime, we have been able to observe with our own eyes how human beings can move from a state of civilization to a state of barbarism and back again to civilization during the period of the two world wars—a mere fifty years. Apparently the residue of primitive instincts exists in all human beings and, given the proper social climate, can be unleashed. We know now where this residue is located in the human mind, and we also know how it can flood feelings and distort thinking.

We are a long way from having learned how to harness this new knowledge and use it for the building of the better society. But there is no doubt that some of this knowledge has already significantly affected our thinking and some of our attitudes, as compared to a century ago. People talk now about subconscious attitudes, about rationalizations, about the rights of infants. There is in the popular attitude some consideration of alternatives, a recognition that we may not have been fully conscious of why we felt this way or acted that way. There is considerably less repetition of old wives' tales about love and hate, sexuality and dirt. There is considerable awareness of the role of the unconscious in our child-rearing attitudes. People take it for granted today that significant developments take place in the individual from birth on; they recognize that there is a body of knowledge about the early years, and it is no coincidence that the most popular books on infant and child care are based on principles that developed from the knowledge of child analysis. That the behavior of adults toward infants may have significant effects on the growing child's personality is today fairly common knowledge, as compared with the past, when the childhood years were regarded as happy play years with no serious troubles to mar the rosy haven of infancy. That pain and confusion can stunt growth in early life is by now part of everyday thinking.

In this sense, psychoanalysis has been one of the important civilizing factors. Its significance lies in the prevention of mental illness. If one considers the fundamental changes in human attitudes that its findings have brought about, and adds to them the demonstrated influence of psychoanalysis on psychiatry, psychotherapy, and mental hygiene, it seems fair to conclude that a science which has made such substantial contributions to human relations and to the deeper understanding of human beings is one of the significant social factors of this century.

SOME NATIONAL ORGANIZATIONS IN THE MENTAL HEALTH FIELD

Of the many national, state, and local organizations in the mental health field, a few have been listed below. While they serve their specific functions, there is also some overlapping among them. Most of them have state or local branches that may be able to give information about:

Mental Health Services: National Association for Mental Health
10 Columbus Circle, New York, N.Y.
Psychoanalytic Services: American Psychoanalytic Association
36 West 44th Street, New York, N.Y.
Psychiatric Services: American Psychiatric Association
1700 18th St., N.W., Washington, D.C.
Psychological Services: American Psychological Association
1333 10th St., N.W., Washington, D.C.
Social Work Services: National Association of Social Workers
95 Madison Avenue, New York, N.Y.
Child Guidance Services: American Orthopsychiatric Association
1790 Broadway, New York, N.Y.
Research Services: National Institute of Mental Health
Bethesda, Maryland

Some Related Reading:

On the HISTORY OF PSYCHOANALYSIS:

ERNEST JONES, *The Life and Work of Sigmund Freud,* 3 vols. New York: Basic Books, 1953.

On TRAINING FOR PSYCHOANALYSIS:

BERTRAM LEWIN AND HELEN ROSS, *Psychoanalytic Education in the United States.* New York: W. W. Norton & Co., 1960.

On the THEORY OF PSYCHOANALYSIS:

ROBERT WAELDER, *Basic Theory of Psychoanalysis.* New York: International Universities Press, 1960.

On the VALIDATION OF PSYCHOANALYSIS:

E. PUMPIAN-MINDLIN, in *Psychoanalysis as a Science.* Stanford, Calif.: Stanford University Press, 1952.

On OTHER FORMS OF THERAPY:

RUTH L. MONROE, *Schools of Psychoanalytic Thought.* New York: Dryden Press, 1955.

On NATIONAL MENTAL HEALTH:

Action for Mental Health: The Report to Congress by the Joint Commission on Mental Illness and Health. New York: Basic Books, 1961.